DREAM BIG
PLAN SMART

Finding Your Pathway to
Level 5 Multiplication

by Todd Wilson

with Will Mancini

Edited by Lindy Lowry
Collaboration with Will Mancini
Foreword by Ralph Moore
Cover design by Karen Pheasant and Don Smith

Dedication

This book is dedicated to the Level 4 and 5 church multipliers who serve on the Becoming Five leadership team. These leaders have been instrumental in developing and bringing clarity to the content in this book. It has been a journey of learning and discovery. These thought leaders have sacrificially invested of their time, talent, and finances to help guide this vitally important conversation.

Special thanks to:

Dave Browning
Wade Burnett
Jeff Christopherson
Bill Couchenour
Bill Easum
Dave Ferguson
Tim Hawks
Daniel Im
Chris Lagerlof
Mac Lake
Mike McDaniel
Ralph Moore
Dave Rhodes
Brian Sanders
Larry Walkemeyer
Tim Wheat
Greg Wiens

This book is also dedicated to all of the courageous leaders who will step out of their comfort zones to surrender and put to death the prevailing Level 3 scorecards, opting instead for the fruit of Level 4 and 5 multiplication!

exponential.org

Special Thanks

Lindy Lowry for her amazing writing and editing skills. This book would not have happened without her long hours and sleepless nights.

Bill Couchenour and Dave Rhodes for their leadership in pulling together and facilitating the national Becoming Five team.

Will Mancini for his insights, tools, and collaboration on this project.

Dave Ferguson for his positivity, encouragement, and passion for seeing the needle on the scorecard of multiplication increase from less than 4% of U.S. churches ever reproducing to greater than 10%.

Ralph Moore for his encouragement, wisdom and role modeling. Thank you for your faithful and persistent passion to see the Church be all she can be.

The entire Exponential Team for sacrificially serving church multiplication leaders, and stepping up to do whatever was needed, whenever it was needed, to finish this resource.

Special Invitation

Please consider attending one of our Exponential 2017 events. Our goal is to help shape your paradigm for multiplication, inspire and encourage you to multiply, and equip you to turn ideas into action. Our 2017 conferences are built on the content of this book, and are designed to help you move from ideas and inspiration to implementation and impact.

2017 Theme: Dream Big: Finding Your Pathway to Level 5 Multiplication.

Location and Dates: Our East and West locations are larger, full-service events with thousands of attendees, 100+ speakers, 20+ tracks, and 150+ workshops. Our Exponential regional events are shorter and geographically based (which translates to lower overall costs for large teams). Regionals bring the full "punch" of the national conferences' five main stage sessions without the breakout workshops.

National Events
Exponential East // Orlando, Florida // April 24 – 27, 2017
Exponential West // Los Angeles // October 2 – 5, 2017

Regional Events
Washington, D.C. // September 11 – 12, 2017
Chicago // November 7 – 8, 2017
Houston, Texas // November 29 – 30, 2017
Seattle, Washington // TBA // check our web site

Special Offer

National Events – Use coupon code DREAMBIG2017 for $39 off the regular rate.
Regional Events – Buy one registration and get one free admission for groups of five or more

Dream Big Workbook

Our supplemental *Dream Big Workbook* is filled with practical exercises and key questions to help you and your team work through the content in this book. Included in it are interactive reflection questions, self-assessment tools, and exercises for pursuing perspective and clarity on your church's current multiplication culture (Actual) and where you want to be in the future (Aspirational).

Will Mancini, co-author (with Warren Bird) of *God Dreams* and collaborator with me on this book, serves as the workbook architect. Will is the best vision clarity specialist I know. He is a master toolmaker and has a profound ability to sniff out clarity.

The workbook follows the same outline as this book, using the vision clarity process from *God Dreams*. We've designed it to be used either individually or in teams. We believe this resource will help you and your team move from a desire for multiplication to developing a vision and strategy for actual implementation.

The *Dream Big Workbook* is available for free download at exponential.org.

Inside

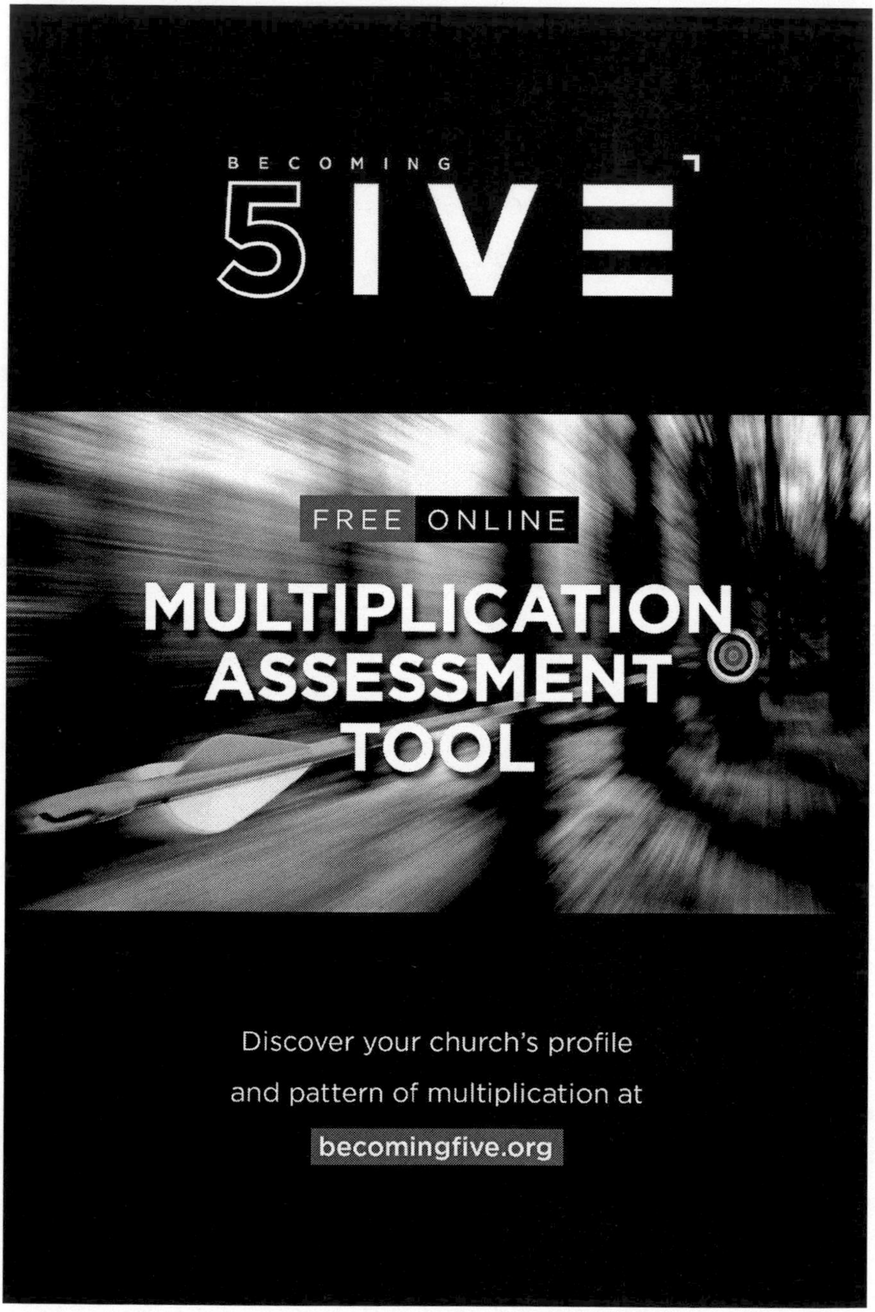
BECOMING
5IVE
FREE ONLINE
MULTIPLICATION ASSESSMENT TOOL
Discover your church's profile and pattern of multiplication at
becomingfive.org

Foreword

We seem to have lost our bearings.

In 2010, a Pew Research study indicated that 55 percent of Millennials view church in a positive light. Today, the same researchers say that number has dropped to 18 percent.

According to the report, Millennials hold the church in lower esteem than tech companies, universities, or labor unions. Churches fared better than big banks or the news media, but that isn't saying much. These stats—despite a lingering interest in Jesus—tell us that we're simply failing to engage the next generation on a meaningful level.

Driven more by relationships and truth than by structures and rules, this generation is ripe for a wave of new churches that operate very differently from the prevailing, familiar form we know.

I believe this paradigm shift is where this new book comes into play. *Dream Big Plan Smart* continues the vital conversation that *Spark* and *Becoming a Level 5 Multiplying Church* started. Todd Wilson, Will Mancini and the Exponential team are rewriting the vocabulary of the church. They've given us a new scorecard for success, and now in this book Todd details the steps we need to change and shape our paradigms around that new scoreboard. It doesn't require much imagination to realize that Exponential is on the leading edge of a critical shift that will dictate the Church's viability with the surrounding culture.

Simply put, we need to multiply more churches if we expect to reach the nooks and crannies of society. Not everyone fits into a Level 3 addition-focused church—as evidenced by the vast majority of Millennials who don't think much of the church. History demonstrates that newly planted churches evangelize best. Reality screams that we need more disciple-making churches.

11

As I read *Dream Big Plan Smart*, I was surprised to learn that Todd lays out the very pathway our church (Hope Chapel) walked, while moving from a single congregation to a church multiplication movement. Even more surprising, Todd presents these principles in roughly the order in which we *stumbled* upon them. We got into this multiplication thing accidentally. This book denies you the luxury of fumbling forward. Disciple making is crucial to church multiplication, and Todd drives that point home, leaving us no wiggle room. I once convinced several large church pastors to launch churches but forgot to teach them to make disciples first. Their failures still haunt me. This book makes no such mistake. The overt goal, plainly stated, is that you choose to make disciples that make disciples and plant churches that plant churches.

Bottom line: You cannot expect to change the world if you don't first *decide* to change the world. But decision-making isn't enough. There is concrete planning to do; inevitably tensions will follow. But as this book points out, multiplication is doable. Jesus has not only commissioned you to make disciples, He has also equipped you and your church for this world-changing mission. Everything I learned by struggling for over a decade and a half is now yours in this well-written book. I encourage you to give yourself a few hours with this book and the supplementary *Dream Big Plan Smart Workbook*, highlighter in hand. Then hang on tight! Your life is about change.

~Ralph Moore, founder of the Level 5 Hope Chapel multiplication movement, which has planted more than 2,000 churches worldwide.

Introduction
Continuing the Conversation...

What will it take to move the multiplication needle from less than 4 percent of U.S. churches ever reproducing to greater than 10 percent?

As a community of activists devoted to church multiplication, Exponential has focused our attention on this critical question. We believe that church multiplication is the best way carry out Jesus' Great Commission to "make disciples to the ends of the earth." We dream of movements characterized by disciples who make disciples who plant churches that plant churches.

Exponential comes alongside church leaders to inspire, challenge and equip them to greater levels of multiplication. We've stewarded the conversation through numerous resources, including two key books: *Spark: Igniting a Culture of Multiplication* and *Becoming a Level 5 Multiplying Church*. In *Spark*, we focused on the value of multiplication and looked at the cultures most churches naturally create. In *Becoming a Level 5 Multiplying Church*, we addressed barriers and introduced a framework of five levels of multiplication. To help churches discover their level of multiplication, we developed a supplementary free online assessment tool (becomingfive.org).

In this next book, we're focusing on helping leaders understand the importance of gaining perspective on their current culture, developing a vision for multiplication, and developing a plan for the future. Before moving forward, it's important to first look back and review what we've covered in recent years.

KEY MULTIPLICATION CONCEPTS
(from *Spark* and *Becoming a Level 5 Multiplying Church*)

3 Key Multiplication Challenges

In *Spark*, we identified three key challenges for the Church as we pursue multiplication:

1.   A growing number of leaders are questioning the quality of our disciple making in the local church. We are not producing an army of fully devoted and surrendered disciples who will go and start new churches as the fruit of disciple making.

2.   Multiplication strategies are by far the minority to addition strategies. Most churches value and default to addition cultures, opting for accumulating more attendees, staff, larger facilities, more sites, etc., rather than creating a culture of releasing and sending. We are building addition capacity, but not multiplication capacity.

3.   The church is one of the best mobilizers of volunteers for service. However, these mobilization strategies are most often focused on feeding the growth of addition capacity rather than helping people live deployed within the sweet spot of their unique calling. We catch and consume rather than develop and deploy.

Add and Multiply

At the core of healthy Kingdom growth is disciple making and sending capacity—disciples who make disciples planting churches that plant churches. In *Spark*, we introduced the following concepts:

1.   Add and Multiply Disciples: We *add* one spiritual infant at a time while we *make and multiply* mature, biblical disciples who reproduce.

14

2. Add and Multiply Sending Capacity: We increase our *local* capacity for making biblical disciples while also creating *Kingdom* capacity for implementing new environments and contexts for biblical disciple making beyond our local church. Our ability to make biblical disciples is the core ingredient needed for increasing sending capacity.

Healthy New Testament culture should occur at the intersection of addition and multiplication. Both must work in tandem. Because we win people to Jesus one by one, we must have a local or "micro" strategy that is reproducible and works at adding the next one. At the same time, we must intentionally have a "macro" strategy for multiplying our impact beyond our local context. The macro strategy recognizes that the most powerful way to multiply is to create new churches that become platforms for addition at the individual believer level. Macro results provide new contexts and frontiers for micro strategies. Local *and* global in harmony. The two must work synergistically with the adding, thereby fueling the multiplying.

If our aligning values and core elements are off center, we see the opposite of both disciple making and sending capacity. Instead of adding and making biblical disciples who reproduce, we make cultural Christians who need to be consistently entertained and fed. Instead of multiplication growth (release and send), we get addition growth (catch and accumulate).

Possibly the single-largest obstacle to multiplication occurs when we position addition activities (new programs and ministries, new facilities, small groups, outreach events, church wide campaigns, etc.) as our primary strategy for growth, rather than seeing these activities as a supporting element to healthy biblical growth and multiplication. Though we increase our effectiveness at adding to our numbers and breaking organizational growth barriers, unfortunately we may be building bigger and bigger holding tanks for cultural Christians.

A Framework and Vocabulary for Multiplication

In *Becoming a Level 5 Multiplying Church*, we introduced a framework and vocabulary to help guide the multiplication conversation. Specifically, we focused on five levels or cultures of multiplication in churches:

Level 1: Subtracting Approximately 80 percent of U.S. churches are subtracting (attendance is decreasing) or have plateaued. These churches live in a survival/scarcity culture that makes it difficult to even *think* about multiplication.

Level 2: Plateaued Churches that are plateaued demonstrate some characteristics of both subtraction and addition cultures. Their thinking lies in a state of tension between scarcity and growth.

Level 3: Adding Some 15 to 20 percent of churches find themselves here. In addition-growth churches, attendance is increasing. Many are often externally focused, making an impact in their surrounding communities, and many have added multi-site venues. For this framework, we intentionally defined churches that have a strong addition-growth culture, yet are not aggressively multiplying, as Level 3 churches. Most of the largest and fastest-growing churches that make our "envy lists" are actually Level 3 churches.

Level 4: Reproducing At this level, approximately 4 percent of U.S. churches reproduce programmatically as part of their growth. While they may aspire to be a multiplying church and may even be making progress in that direction, too often the tensions and forces pulling them back to Level 3 limit their ability to move more fully to Level 5. Because multiplication is not yet strongly embedded in their DNA, it won't happen spontaneously without programming.

Level 5: Multiplying Currently represented by less than .005 percent of U.S. churches, multiplying churches focus more on sending and releasing than catching and accumulating. They plant churches as a regular part of their existence. Level 5 church leaders see their church through a Kingdom lens. Their burden is more for Kingdom capacity than for local church capacity.

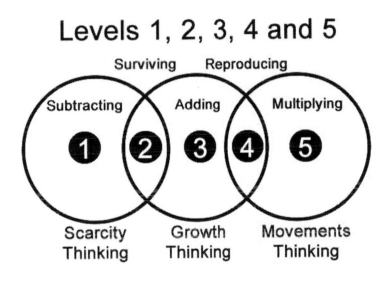

Creating a Multiplication Culture

Our core values and convictions are always transforming our thinking into action. The key question is, "What culture are you creating?" Are you developing a subtraction, survival and scarcity culture ("We will [fill in the blank] after we grow or can afford it")? An addition culture focused on an insatiable drive for breaking the next growth barrier ("Where is the next one?")? Or are you bucking the norm and creating a multiplication culture ("Thy Kingdom, not my kingdom")?

Currently, the prevailing growth culture in today's churches is addition with most leaders measuring their success by weekend attendance growth.

In *Spark,* we looked at how culture is created through the alignment of three factors: core values, narratives, and behaviors.

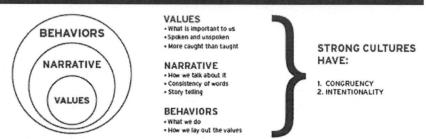

Here's a quick synopsis:

1. Our *core values* reflect what we really care about deep down. They are the things so important to us that they shape our thoughts and our actions. Our values overflow to shape the words of our mouth (our narrative) and the actions of our hands (our behaviors).

2. Our *narratives* are shaped by the language we use, the stories we tell, and how frequently we talk about and celebrate the things most important to us. Our narratives inspire others to embrace our values and engage on common mission with us.

3. Our *behaviors* are the things we actually do, including how and where we invest the time, talent, and financial resources entrusted to our care.

Rethinking the Operating System

The prevailing operating systems that give us church growth are falling short of giving us church multiplication. The operating system (the OS) in your computer or smart phone provides the platform for the launch of thousands of possible applications. Basically, the OS determines if you can run certain apps.

Right now, our operating system in the Church is perfectly aligned to give us what we're getting. The current system sets its sights on accumulation and addition growth. And while we are adding, we aren't adding in a way that produces the transformation needed for multiplication. Instead, the best pathway to a multiplication culture is built on the foundation of disciples who mature and make additional disciples. The bottom line is that we need to rethink our current operating systems and become courageous leaders willing to discover and embrace new systems that set us up for multiplication.

Internal and External Tensions

The journey toward multiplication is filled with external and internal tensions. Regardless of your church's current level of multiplication, you will have tension. In *Spark*, we highlighted nearly 20 different multiplication tensions that churches might face in moving from Levels 1, 2 and 3 to Levels 4 and 5. However, nearly all of those tensions find their roots in three common factors: our motives, our measurements and our methods. Below is a short description of each one:

1.   *Tension of motives (here or there?)*: This tension is rooted in our definition of success. Is our vision limited to accumulating and growing larger *here* (where we are), or is it balanced with an equal focus and passion for sending *there* (the next church)? All leaders live in the tension between being *here* and being *there*, with almost everything pulling them toward *here*. To move through this tension, we must embrace and become passionate about the value of multiplication. We must balance *here* and *there*.

2.   *Tension of measurement (grow or send?)*: This tension is rooted in where we prioritize our focus: Where do we focus our time, talent and treasure? Growing *here* or sending *there*? The same staff and finances that can help us grow *here* are the ones

needed to send *there*. As our local platform increases, our capacity for even greater sending grows.

3.   *Tension of methods (safety or risk?)*: At the core of this tension is how we allocate our time (activities), talents (leadership), and treasures (finances) to building local *and* Kingdom capacity. What will we actually *do* and what hard decisions will we make to become a Level 5 multiplying church? Good intentions will not move you from Level 1 to 5.

To overcome the Level 3 addition-growth scorecard, we must embrace new motives, measures and methods and be courageous change makers.

Looking Ahead

The strong addition culture that pulls a Level 3 church toward greater levels of addition growth is the very culture that inhibits a church from moving to greater levels of multiplication (Levels 4 and 5). The financial and leadership resources required to feed Level 3 are the same resources needed to fuel multiplication in Levels 4 and 5. When this tyranny of the "or" emerges, addition growth usually wins out over multiplication.

You're likely reading this book because you instinctively know that addition scorecards are winning out over multiplication. You know down deep that something is wrong with the values, narratives and behaviors that have proven successful in our generation for building a successful addition-focused church. Like thousands of other church leaders and a growing number of your peers, you may be experiencing a discontent or even a crisis of faith that's hard to articulate.

If you are ready to move forward with a vision and strategy for multiplication, this new book is for you! Let's press into your church's specific journey and consider the vision, perspective and strategy you need on your pathway to multiplication.

Chapter 1
Preparation: Mapping the Journey

"Would you tell me, please, which way I ought to go from here?" said Alice.
"That depends a good deal on where you want to get to," said the Cat.
"I don't much care where—" said Alice,
"Then it doesn't matter which way you go," said the Cat.
"–so long as I get somewhere," Alice added as an explanation.
"Oh, you're sure to do that," said the Cat, "if you only walk long enough."
~*Alice's Adventures in Wonderland* by Lewis Carroll

From this classic exchange between Alice and the Cheshire Cat, we get the often cited paraphrase, "If you don't know where you're going, any road will get you there." Or, a better phrase when it comes to church multiplication might be, "If you've selected the wrong destination, you will never experience the better dreams God has for you at the right destination."

Before the merger of smart phones and GPS, we had good old-fashioned printed maps. They filled our car's glove compartment and the spaces under our seats. They folded up like a complex, trick accordion. Most were outdated by the time you bought them. They were cumbersome and slow, generally unbearable for the directionally challenged. But those maps were a vital tool for preparing for long trips and vacations. They forced us to have the discipline to discern where we currently were, where we desired to be, and the best pathway to get to our destination.

The wonderful thing about modern GPS navigational systems is that you only need to know your destination to find your way. Simply enter (or speak) an address and *voila*, you have voice-guided directions to your destination. No worries if you're lost, uncertain of the barriers that will slow you down (e.g., traffic or construction), or lack familiarity with the landmarks along the way. Give the GPS an address, and you're on your way! The GPS does the hard work, including making needed course corrections and "rerouting" us. You need very little preparation and planning to get where you want to go.

If only our journey toward multiplication were this simple. Just plug in your desired destination and set the autopilot. Unfortunately, it doesn't work that way. There is no bypassing the hard work of understanding where we want to go; gaining perspective on where we are; plotting a thoughtful course to get there; and then managing that journey.

You're probably reading this book because you genuinely want to see your church multiply. You sense that things are not the way you'd like them to be, yet you're unsure of how to change them. You're also probably keenly aware that the cultural changes will be difficult—understanding that there's a reason less than 4 percent of U.S. churches ever reproduce and less than 0.1 percent multiply.

In this first chapter, I offer a basic overview of the elements of strategic planning while chapters 2 through 8 guide you through the process of moving from a *desire* for multiplication to a *dream* for multiplication and ultimately to a *plan* for multiplication.

Vision, Perspective and Strategy

If you're serious about becoming a Level 4 or 5 multiplying church, you need to engage the process. First, you must do the hard work of developing a vision for multiplication. But then the real work begins. You'll have to pack your bags and move beyond the safe land of vision and good intentions to dwell in a place far more uncertain and uncomfortable—the land of perspective and planning. Here is where you'll gain perspective on the realities of your current situation and then plot a course to a better future. As the journey progresses, you'll also need to continually monitor and adjust your strategy or plan for getting there.

Think about the process of putting together a puzzle. Each step allows us to see the process of aligning vision, perspective and strategy.

Gaining Perspective

In embarking on any new journey, we start with the end in mind: a vision. The front of the puzzle box shows you your end goal. The end picture is why you bought the puzzle in the first place. Something about the image attracted you. In the same way, vision shows you a compelling picture of your destination—where you'd like to be in the future. We desire to see the beauty of the completed picture in full, vibrant color. My guess is that the picture of your preferred future is likely different from the one you're currently living. So how do you discover and awaken a new vision for multiplication?

In chapter 2, we're talking about the factors that shape and enable our vision. Part of preparation is ensuring that your vision is rooted in the reality of who your church is (identity) and why your church exists (purpose). Who we are and why we exist are powerful shaping factors for pursuing vision. They're like the rudder on a boat. No matter how enthusiastically you want to get to a specific place across the lake, you'll never get there if the rudder is aligned to a different location. Our core identity and purpose align us to our future destination. However, the only core purpose and identity that will align your church to healthy church multiplication is biblical disciple making.

In chapter 3, we're focusing on the importance of perspective. Like all good things in life, seeing the fruition of a godly vision takes hard work, which starts with gaining perspective on our past and present conditions. We need to ask difficult and probing questions: Where are we? How did we get to this place on our journey? What motivates us? What causes us to celebrate? What causes us to lose sleep? What constrains us? Why do we want a new destination characterized by a multiplication culture? Compared with our desired vision for a better future, what is our actual starting point today?

Before the current era of the GPS, the only way to discern your pathway to a destination on the printed map was to know and understand your starting point. No matter how compelling the destination, you simply could not get there without knowing your current location. Even in today's most advanced GPS systems, the internal workings must first determine your current position before they can guide you to your new destination. Moreover, the GPS must continually gain perspective throughout the trip, comparing where you currently are to where you need to be. Perspective is essential to adjustment, and continual adjustment directs us forward toward our destination.

Lack of perspective may be the biggest obstacle to developing and achieving a realistic but big vision. Let me suggest the following posture for finding perspective:

1. Don't be defensive. Seek truth via facts. Then face those facts with a posture of humility and learning. Intentionally seek to understand your history and how that history has brought you to the church culture you have today. It's important to realize that your current culture is the product of your past. What needs to change in your current culture to redefine the fruit of your church's multiplication future? Be relentless in asking questions and probing for answers. Try pretending that you're a doctor, diagnosing, analyzing and investigating the culture of your church.

2. Use the framework of questions and characteristics of church multiplication culture presented throughout the rest of this book and in the supplemental workbook. Exponential has done part of the hard work for you in developing a list of characteristics and questions that will give you a framework for finding perspective. Take advantage of this framework. Use it.

3. Find perspective before planning. Avoid the temptation to jump ahead to vision and strategy before doing the hard work of gaining

perspective. Work through the questions in this book and the workbook, both individually and with your team. Build a solid foundation of understanding for your future vision and strategy. Use the framework of questions, characteristics and the perspective you gain to help shape your vision for multiplication.

Building Vision and Strategy

Chapter 4 moves us to the importance of and need for a clear vision for multiplication. Without vision, we'll never get to multiplication. In fact, Exponential believes so strongly in vision that we devoted our 2017 theme to it. "Dream Big" is all about the importance of a committed and strong vision for multiplication.

Vision and big dreams inspire and excite us, but as you probably already know, vision doesn't get anything accomplished on its own. For most church leaders, vision is where they start ... and, unfortunately... stay. What happens when we continue to admire the picture on the puzzle box with good intentions to put it together but never actually get started? Obviously, the puzzle remains unassembled; the image is never completed. The puzzle pieces lying in front of us never become the picture on the box.

In chapters 5 and 6, I focus on helping you understand the key pathways to multiplication and developing a strategy or plan. If we have a clear vision for where we'd like to be in the future and a comprehensive understanding of where we are today, our strategy emerges as the pathway from today's reality to tomorrow's dream. There is typically no one right or perfect pathway or strategy. Just as a GPS often has several possible routes to our destination, our pathways to multiplication are many. The key is selecting one and then diligently implementing it.

In our puzzle analogy, strategy represents the approach we take in assembling the pieces. We may find the four corner pieces; separate and assemble all of the edge pieces for the frame; segregate the pieces with similar colors; or focus on distinct objects and colors on each puzzle piece. In our church, our strategies often reflect the natural rhythms and realities of our unique culture (DNA) and how we work. Understanding how your church is wired will help you 1) discern if you need rewiring; and 2) identify a unique plan for your context.

In Chapter 7, I'm asking you to count the cost of what it will take to move toward a multiplication vision for your church, thinking through the magnitude and deep implications of what it will mean for you personally to change your church's scorecard and current culture. Part of gaining perspective is turning from what we now know is wrong to what we understand to be right.

In chapter 8, we'll look at priorities and what's important now to build momentum. Once we have a plan for where we want to go, continual honest assessment of how we're doing compared with our vision and plan is essential. Day after day, we must seek perspective, adjusting our strategy as necessary, to get us to the right destination—the place where God awakens big dreams.

Let's get started…

Chapter 2
Purpose
Why Do We Exist?

"Go and make disciples of all nations, baptizing them in the name of the Father and of the Son and of the Holy Spirit, and teaching them to obey everything I have commanded you" (Matt. 28:19-20).

~ Jesus

Known as the father of modern management and author of more than 30 books, Peter Drucker understood the importance of an organization understanding its mission. In one of his most powerful (and shortest) books, *The Five Most Important Questions You Will Ever Ask About Your Organization*, Drucker said that the first and most important question is, "What is your mission?" or "What is your core business?" or "Why do you exist?"

"The mission says why you do what you do," Drucker explained, "not the means by which you do it."[1]

He was equally passionate that the "how of what you do" naturally flows from a clear and succinct core mission. Drucker, who devoted a great deal of his time helping churches, believed strongly that "the plan begins with a mission," and that a fundamental responsibility of leadership is to make sure everybody knows the mission, understands it, and lives it.

So in the Church, what is our purpose or mission? Another way of asking that question is, "Why do we do what we do?" and, "In the end, what do we want to be remembered for?" Our answer to all of these questions must be a resounding call: *biblical disciple making*. Any other core mission will take us off track and fail to lead to healthy church multiplication and movements. If we want to establish a culture and vision for multiplication that can be understood and lived out, we must start by ensuring our core purpose or mission is biblically correct and is actually capable of producing healthy multiplication.

As founder of the Hope Chapel Movement, Ralph Moore knows a thing or two about making disciples. Starting from 12 people in 1971, Hope Chapel movement has now seen more than 2,300 churches planted to date—making it one of the few Level 5 churches in the United States.

"Disciple making is at the heart of Hope Chapel," Moore says. "I'd say that making disciples is 90 percent of this movement."

Moore shares an early story from his denominational days. Known as the "church planting guy" in the denomination, Moore worked hard to convince large churches in the denomination to plant churches.

"They did. They poured resources into all of these churches—more resources than we had—and most failed. I had gotten everyone in our denomination revved up about planting a church and quickly realized that was the wrong thing to do because they didn't have disciple making as their core. They weren't making disciples. Disciple making is critical to multiplication. At the very beginning, we started discipling people and saw them disciple others."

Think about the huge stadium events Jesus could have filled or the giant megachurch He could have led or the international network He could have handed off to others. But Jesus' command was clear: "Go and make disciples." For three years on earth, He modeled disciple making and made disciple makers. He then commanded them to do the same. When He completed His work here, Jesus told His disciples, "As the father has sent me, I am sending you" (John 20:21). Soon thereafter, He gave His Great Commission to go and make disciples to the ends of the earth.

So our mission or purpose is clear (and it meets Drucker's well-known requirement that it fits on a T-shirt): "Disciple making!" or "Making Disciple Makers!" To more fully capture the sending or "go" impulse of our Founder's command, we could also expand the purpose: *Make disciples who make disciples that plant churches that plant churches.*

Assuming we embrace this core purpose, the most important question then is, "What type of disciples are we making?" Are we producing biblical disciples who make disciples that plant churches that plant churches? Or are we largely making cultural Christians that feed our numerical growth, but don't make disciples who multiply? Are we producing followers who are fully surrendered and put Jesus at the center of their lives—their priorities, their family, their work, their money, etc.—or are we simply convincing people to believe in Jesus but not surrender to His Lordship? Are we mobilizing a movement of missionaries to carry the fullness of Jesus into every crack and cranny of society, or are we growing an army of church attendees who give an hour of themselves each week?

These questions are tough but important ones to confront. Contemplating and answering them is essential to establishing the foundation necessary for multiplication. *Is biblical disciple making really the core that drives what you do as a church and how you do everything you do?*

Disciple Making: The First and Critical Dimension of Multiplication
(Creating a Culture of Disciple Making)

At the core of any multiplication movement is disciple making. The general or common calling shared by all Christians, everywhere, throughout all time, is to follow Jesus' command that we be disciples who make disciples wherever we are! In his letter to the church in Ephesus, Paul tells us that we are called to have the fullness of Jesus in us and to carry that fullness to others as we make disciples, wherever we find ourselves. If we want to understand why we aren't seeing movements of exponential multiplication in the West, we should start by looking at the quality of our disciple making.

Adding and multiplying disciples

We can look at disciple making through the lens of adding disciples (making converts) and reproducing disciples (making disciples of others). The pathways for adding disciples— connecting with people, introducing them to Jesus, and bringing them to a point of accepting Him as Lord—are the entry point to making biblical disciples.

Adding Disciples ←——————————————→ **Multiplying Disciples**

Regardless of our specific strategies, models and approaches, we add people to the movement of Christianity one follower at a time. We can't change that, nor should we try. It's how our Founder designed it to be. Infants in the faith spiritually mature and then reproduce themselves, repeating the cycle. The "adding" and the "making" work together. Those far from God become disciples who give their full devotion to becoming more like Jesus and having His fullness in them. In the process of becoming more mature disciples, they naturally make disciples of others— multiplying themselves in others. Disciples who make disciples the way Jesus did are the fuel of multiplication movements.

Unfortunately, in our addition-oriented growth cultures, we hijack this natural method. Consider these three tensions:

1.   We replace (rather than supplement) the adding with our man-made growth strategy methods (for example, outreach, marketing, Sunday services, programs, great preaching, etc.).

2.   Many churches struggle with evangelism versus discipleship. Some churches become so focused on corporate pre-evangelism efforts to make converts that disciple making never becomes embedded into the church's DNA. You might call it a significant imbalance between evangelism and discipleship versus a balanced and integrated approach. In his

free eBook, *Disciplism*, Alan Hirsch says we need to reframe evangelism within the context of discipleship.

"We must not stop sharing the Good News, but here's the deal: Evangelism gets done along the way as we do discipleship," Hirsch explains. "The Great Commission is just about discipling the nations. Know what happens? As you disciple people, evangelism takes place because it's done in the context of discipleship."[2]

3.   Finally, we struggle with the tension between making biblical disciples and cultural Christians. Is it possible that we think we're focusing on Jesus and making biblical disciples when in actuality we're focusing on making cultural Christians? A normal part of the maturation process of biblical disciples is making other disciples. One becomes many. Contrast that with cultural Christians. They consume. Add one and continue having to feed them to keep them happy. When spiritual infants never fully mature and reproduce, cultural Christianity breaks the natural reproduction cycle. To compensate, we wind up doubling down on our addition-growth strategies (marketing, outreach, programs, etc.). The insanity occurs when we double our efforts to keep adding more to increase our numbers. If our standard is accumulating large numbers of spiritual seekers and cultural Christians without equal diligence to make biblical disciples that make disciples, we will be sorely disappointed in our lack of multiplication.

By making biblical disciples, we become more effective at carrying the fullness of Jesus into every corner of our communities, ultimately sending disciples to go and multiply new churches that create even greater capacity for healthy Kingdom growth. Making cultural Christians also scales our efforts— unfortunately with sideways energy that shunts our multiplication capacity.

In his seminal work, *The Forgotten* Ways, Alan Hirsch identifies six elements in multiplication movements (what he calls mDNA). The first two elements, he says, are "Jesus is Lord" and "disciple making." Hirsch's take on these two elements is not for the faint of heart. He passionately advocates for a whole-hearted, radical surrender to Jesus with disciple making permeating all we say and do.

"Many of our current practices seem to be the wrong way around," Hirsch says. "We seem to make church complex and discipleship too easy. Christianity without discipleship is always Christianity without Christ."[3]

Disciple making is absolutely critical to Level 5 multiplication both in your church and the Church at large. Our supplemental *Dream Big Workbook* is filled with exercises and questions to help you assess where your church currently is (Actual) and where you want to be (Aspirational). It includes a list of questions for assessing how your church is doing at living out our core purpose of disciple making. Download this FREE resource at exponential.org.

Building Capacity for Disciple Making: The Second Dimension of Multiplication
(Creating a Culture of Multiplication)

So we've established that our core mission is healthy disciple making (adding and making biblical disciples), and that healthy disciple making is the vital foundation to Level 5 multiplication. But disciple making on its own does not guarantee multiplication. We also need to build the infrastructure necessary to expand and support our disciple-making context.

Capacity is a physical characteristic that enables future growth. Consider the bones in our bodies. They increase in size as you grow. Why? It takes larger bones to support a larger body. Our bones are one key element of how the body naturally builds capacity to support future growth. The larger our bones, the more size and weight we can support.

Every church (and organization) builds capacity. It's natural. However, the key question is, "What type of capacity are we building?"

Think about how Jesus spent three years building the core capacity for the greatest movement in history. By embedding the gospel DNA for disciple making into 12 followers surrendered to His Lordship, He built capacity. Those 12 leaders passed along the genetic code to others who did the same for others in their path. The right capacity for the right motives built into a small band of believers can change the world.

Don't miss this subtle, but profound truth: Each believer has the capacity for multiplication movements. However, the capacity for sustaining these movements, via the local church, must be managed through human hands. In His wisdom, God gave us the Church—in part because we are designed to function like a family, and also to provide us with a platform of capacity for 1) increasing our effectiveness in disciple making, and 2) scaling or multiplying our efforts at disciple making (beyond what unaffiliated, lone ranger disciples can do when they're separated from biblical fellowship).

The institutional part of church, including its infrastructure, processes and resources, is vital to multiplying and sustaining your church's growth via disciple making.

Adding Kingdom Capacity

Although multiplication is built on a healthy foundation of addition, we get in trouble when we focus exclusively (or primarily) on addition capacity, neglecting or limiting multiplication capacity. As you read through the rest of this chapter, pay close attention to the balancing act necessary for managing addition and multiplication factors.

33

Addition Capacity ⟵⟶ **Multiplication Capacity**

Addition capacity represents everything we do to build and grow a local church and impact a local geographic area. Multiplication capacity represents everything we do for making biblical disciples beyond a specific local church.

Think about all of the activities a local church can do to create local capacity for adding numbers locally (regardless of the activity's effectiveness at producing biblical disciples). The list includes but isn't limited to new worships services, new facilities, new staff, new programs, new sites, marketing, outreach, leadership development systems, etc.

Yes, local capacity is vital to healthy growth. There's nothing wrong with initiating or participating in any of these activities. These activities build a solid base for expanding our multiplication activities. But possibly the single-largest obstacle to multiplication occurs when we position addition-capacity activities as our primary strategy for growth, rather than seeing them as a supporting element to healthy disciple making.

Too many churches have unintentionally put addition capacity and strategies as the target of their growth efforts. The result? Though we increase our effectiveness at breaking organizational growth barriers and adding to our numbers, the unfortunate reality is that we may be building bigger and bigger holding tanks for cultural Christians.

In the words of C.S. Lewis: "There exists in every church something that sooner or later works against the very purpose for which it came into existence. So we must strive very hard, by the grace of God to keep the church focused on the mission that Christ originally gave to it."[4]

Though we do definitely need it, addition capacity is not the most leveraged form of capacity building. The process of building multiplication capacity creates Kingdom capacity for implementing new environments and contexts for biblical disciple making. This key element requires that we release and send leaders, dollars and support to start new communities of faith that are not directly under our control and authority.

Think about it this way. Where addition capacity focuses on increasing the capacity to grow trees in our own orchard, multiplication capacity focuses on planting new orchards. We need both. Addition systems and activities enhance healthy multiplication. For example, we can use the same leadership development systems that support local church capacity expansion to develop and deploy church planters.

Most of the behavioral characteristics of multiplying churches require that we move beyond an adding-accumulating focus to a releasing-sending focus.

FREE Church Assessment on Capacity Building

Before continuing, spend 30 minutes taking the FREE online church multiplication assessment available at www.becomingfive.org. The assessment measures your church's cultural capacity for multiplication. You'll receive immediate results, including a Multiplication Score (Level 1 through 5) and a Multiplication Pattern.

NOTE: This tool is one of three that Exponential is developing to give leaders a more holistic view of multiplication culture. The three assessment tools focus on: your disciple-making culture (the critical element); capacity building or multiplication culture; and mobilization or empowering culture (discussed in the next section below). The current assessment available at www.becomingfive.org focuses exclusively on your capacity and culture for multiplication. Taking the capacity assessment will give you a better context for completing the Perspectives questions in the *Dream Big Workbook*.

Enter your assessment scores below:

My Multiplication
Capacity Score: Level 1   2   3   4   5

My Multiplication
Capacity Pattern: _____

After completing the assessment, you'll want to work through the Perspectives questions on capacity building in our supplemental *Dream Big Workbook* (free download via exponential.org).

Mobilizing Disciples to Make Disciples:
The Third Dimension of Multiplication
(Creating a Culture of Empowerment and Mobilization)

We will always have healthy tension between adding disciples (making converts) and making multiplying disciples (growing and reproducing mature believers), as well as a tension between building capacity for local addition growth and building capacity for Kingdom multiplication. Your role as a leader is to simultaneously manage the tensions in these two dimensions. You might say that we need the genius of the *"and"* in both disciple making *and* capacity building!

But these two key dimensions are not enough to fulfill Jesus' command to "go." We must also *mobilize* disciples to carry the fullness of Jesus into every corner of society as they make disciples. We must have a culture of empowerment where the fruit of mature disciple making is disciples who *go*.

In his letter to the church in Ephesus, Paul connects the dots for us, showing us how we fit into the disciple-making mission of the

Church. In the opening chapter, he offers a great description of the potential of the Church, essentially saying that we (the Church) have the capacity to carry (or to be) the fullness of Jesus into every crack and cranny of society. In the second chapter, he tells us that we are each a unique creation with a specific role to play in carrying the fullness of Jesus to society. And in the fourth chapter, Paul notes that Jesus Himself has equipped each of us with specific gifts to play our unique roles in the mission. To fulfill our mission, we must *mobilize* and *go*!

Mobilization gives us two simultaneous tensions to manage. Scripture calls us to "live in common" as a family of believers *and* to simultaneously "live deployed" as missionaries in our unique corners of society. My book, *More: Find Your Personal Calling and Live Life to the Fullest Measure*, addresses this mobilization dimension in more detail.

As I researched calling, I learned that church historians look at personal calling through two lenses. The first is what they call "common" or general calling. We share this calling with all Christians. For example, Jesus has called us to be disciples who make disciples wherever we are. We are also to be healthy functioning children in God's family via the church community. Like the church in Acts 2, we are to "live in common." Look at the collective "they" statements we find in Acts 2:46-47:

They met daily.
They broke bread together.
They had everything in common.
They sold property and possessions to give to those in need.

The last part of verse 47 tells us: "… and the Lord added to their number daily those who were being saved." We see corporate behaviors leading to personal salvations. But it was what individuals were doing together, to and for each other—and not what the institution was doing to or for its members. "They" activities are at the heart of corporate macro-addition capacity and of living in common.

The second lens of personal calling is a specific calling that equips each follower of Jesus to play a unique missionary role in carrying the fullness of Jesus into every crack and cranny of society. We each have a mission field of influence and a specific gifting. We are to "live deployed" via that unique calling.

In his book, *Real-Time Connections: Linking Your Job With God's Global Work*, Northwood Church planter/pastor Bob Roberts Jr., shares the insights he gleaned when he realized God has called the whole Church—not just vocational missionaries—to live deployed.

"Rather than encouraging people to use their vocations to serve the church, what if we made it the church's task to mobilize Christians to use their everyday vocations to serve people in need—both locally and globally?" Roberts writes. "What would happen if Christians used their jobs, skills and passions to directly answer Christ's call to minister to those in need? What if we started to feed the hungry, clothe the naked, minister to the oppressed, and shelter the homeless? Could this be God's plan for reaching the nations and fulfilling the Great Commission?"[5]

This seismic shift in thinking inverted the church's approach to evangelism: "Instead of focusing on building a church by bringing people into it," Roberts writes, "we focused on being missionaries to our area, making disciples who would fill churches."[6]

Living in common vs. living deployed

This command of living in common while living deployed often creates a tension in our churches. We need people to use their gifts as part of our addition-capacity activities. Our local church needs greeters, ushers, a set-up and teardown team, small group leaders, nursery workers, student ministry volunteers, hospitality teams, etc. However, in our zeal to create addition-growth capacity and "feed the beast," we often miss or even mute this dimension of "living deployed" to "release the beast." The average church doesn't see equipping and mobilizing people to *go* and be missionaries in their communities as their role.

An aircraft carrier is a nearly perfect metaphor for understanding the tension between living in common and living deployed. An aircraft carrier's mission is to send air power to places the carrier cannot go; the aircraft are the tip of the sword. Take away the planes, and the carrier is simply floating metal. Dead weight. To carry out that mission, 5,000 men and women work, eat, and do life together—on a common mission, but each with unique roles. Out of that 5,000, only 120 fly the planes. Another 4,800 people cook, clean, and operate machinery in support of the 120 pilots. In the same way, the average church has an army of volunteers living in common to support the work of the paid, full-time professional pastors (the pilots).

This is not the way Jesus intended the Church to function. Using the aircraft carrier metaphor, we are each to live in common, doing whatever is needed to support the family, while simultaneously flying our planes into our unique corners of society. When we don't use our unique calling and gifts to *go*—to deploy into every corner of society—we negatively impact Jesus' mission for His Church. We must find ways to lead our churches in such a way that we're simultaneously living in common *and* living deployed.

The supplemental *Dream Big Workbook* includes a list of questions to help you assess your current culture of empowerment and mobilization. To get more use and application out of this book, it's a good idea to work through the questions in chapter 2 of the workbook before moving ahead.

Perspective on the U.S. Church

Pulling the elements of disciple making, capacity building and mobilization (all discussed in this chapter) into one picture, we can create a "tension" diagram showing how all three elements interact.

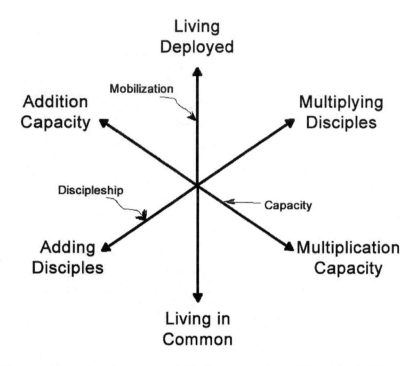

Three of the six elements of the framework (adding disciples, adding addition capacity, and living in common) are addition-oriented. The other three elements (multiplying disciples, building multiplication capacity, and living deployed) are multiplication-oriented.

The core dimensions of multiplication—disciple making, capacity building and mobilization—require an intentional, disciplined balancing act to ensure we manage the tensions at each end to give us the genius of the *and*. We need to add disciples *and* multiply disciples; build addition capacity *and* build multiplication capacity; and we need to live in common *and* live deployed.

With less than 4 percent of U.S. churches ever reproducing, we can assume that churches are not balancing the addition elements with the multiplication elements to get both addition *and* multiplication.

Drawing from each of the elements above as outlined in this chapter, chapter 2 of the supplemental *Dream Big Workbook* includes an entire section to help you see how each of these elements works together for the core purpose of making, multiplying and mobilizing disciples. The workbook also includes questions for you to work through individually and as a team to assess how you're doing with balancing the addition and multiplication dimensions of the framework.

A shared understanding of perspective—where we are today and how we got here—is vital to building a shared vision and strategy for multiplication that everyone owns. Hang in there. The effort you put into looking for perspective will pay off in helping you create a more realistic vision and strategy for multiplication in later chapters. In the next chapter, we continue the process of finding perspective and building on the 3D framework from this chapter.

exponential.org

Chapter 3
Perspective
Where Are We Now?

"Suppose one of you wants to build a tower. Won't you first sit down and estimate the cost to see if you have enough money to complete it?" (Luke 14:28)
~ Jesus

"Human beings are poor examiners, subject to superstition, bias, prejudice, and a profound tendency to see what they want to see rather than what is really there."[1] ~ M. Scott Peck, *The Road Less Traveled*

The past is our best teacher for the future.

Consider the unique story God is writing in each of us. Our lives are like books with chapters, sections, themes, sub-themes, protagonists, antagonists, etc. Keeping with the literary theme, our previous chapters foreshadow our future. For example, looking at the first 25 chapters of our lives will be the best way to gain perspective into what chapters 26 and 27 have in store for us.

We look back to gain perspective on how we've gotten to where we are today and where our current pathway seems to be naturally taking us. If we want to change our future course, we must start that process by understanding and gaining perspective on where we currently are and how we got there. The key question, then, is, "How do we gain perspective?"

Think about how physicians make a diagnosis. My family doctor sees more than 30 patients a day with the average appointment being about 10 to 15 minutes long. Rarely in over 20 years has he been unable to make the right diagnosis within those 10 to 15 minutes. Physicians are masters at getting perspective, quickly! They know how to gather relevant data and compare that data to how things should be. To gain perspective, they use a number of simple tools, such as family history, pulse and blood pressure stats, listening to the heart and lungs, lab tests, scans, etc.

Medical perspective comes by comparing how things are today to how they should be. Doctors also glean perspective by looking at how variables have changed over time from past to present.

So what does it look like for us to assume the role of physician, diagnosing our past and current church multiplication culture? What information is most relevant for us to study, and how do we get started?

In the last chapter, we looked at the core purpose of the Church and used three dimensions of a healthy church multiplication culture as a framework for gaining perspective on our core purpose. By now, you should know that having a strong core purpose rooted in biblical disciple making is a non-negotiable factor in becoming a healthy, Level 5 multiplying church. In this chapter, we're continuing the process of finding perspective to help you establish a firm foundation for creating a vision and strategy for multiplication.

Getting Started

After taking the free, online church multiplication assessment (www.becomingfive.org), the first question most church leaders ask is, "What do I need to do to become a Level 5 multiplying church?" Said differently, "How do we move from where we are today with an addition-growth focus to where we'd like to be in the future with a multiplication culture?"

In writing *Spark* and *Becoming a Level 5 Multiplying Church*, the lack of Level 5 benchmark churches limited our ability to quantitatively define Level 5 church characteristics. We did our best to offer a qualitative description, knowing we would need to continually refine and flesh out the key characteristics of Level 5 churches. We are still earnestly seeking to do that. Unfortunately, we lack solid role models in the United States to learn from and emulate. You might say that we're learning to fly as we fly.

To steward the multiplication conversation and better define the five levels of multiplication, Exponential formed a working team of national leaders from various multiplication ministries and Level 4 and 5 churches. We meet several times throughout the year to focus on the characteristics of Level 5 churches. The team is making solid progress. The next section introduces 10 key values that this team believes are embedded in the culture of Level 5 multiplying churches.

10 Characteristics of a Level 5 Culture

Read through each of the following 10 characteristics carefully. Avoid the temptation to skim the title or a few sentences and assume your church already embraces and practices these values. I encourage you to earnestly seek to understand the core of each characteristic and how these values differ from the values and actions of the average addition-focused church. The supplemental *Dream Big Workbook* includes a tool to help you assess how your church is doing with these characteristics. I strongly encourage you to work through the assessment with your team.

Jesus is Lord: In Level 5 churches, Jesus is the Alpha and Omega, the beginning and the end. Only Jesus brings all things into perspective and gives us the motive and reason for doing all that we do. Our vision, mission, values and strategy all find their authority and context in Jesus. Level 5 churches create cultures where surrender to Jesus' Lordship is central and vital to everything else. Helping people trust and follow Jesus more—including increasing surrender to His Lordship and teaching—lies at the heart of what makes Level 5 churches tick. These churches are serious about Jesus' command to make disciples.

Culture/community of biblical disciple making: Disciple making is key to Level 5 multiplication. In fact, a Level 5 multiplying church is a disciple-making "engine," fueled by the belief and reality that everyone is a biblical disciple maker who reproduces disciples—missionaries mobilized on calling (or unique gifting).

In a Level 5 church, the end goal is reproducing disciples in community (not isolation) and in an ecosystem that integrates evangelism and discipleship. As we disciple individuals, God wholeheartedly activates their impulse to "go" (whether that's planting a church, being part of a new church plant, leading in a missional community, engaging people in their neighborhood or workplace, or becoming a global missionary)! A Level 5 church pursues a disciple-making culture that says, "You can do it; we can help."

Like Ralph Moore's Hope Chapel Movement, Real Life Ministries founded by Jim Putman holds up disciple making above everything else the church does. In an interview with Exponential, Putman talked about how RLM's disciple-making culture continuously births small groups that plant autonomous churches.

"For me, it's not just about how many people are coming, but how many of our people are helping others to know Jesus Christ," says Putman, author of *DiscipleShift*, Exponential's 2012 theme book. "We also ask, 'How many people are in relationship with each other, disciples making disciple makers?' The more disciple makers we are training and releasing, the deeper everything else goes."

New metrics/scorecard: In a Level 5 multiplying church, the conventional definition of "success" gets turned on its proverbial ear. Thus, the priorities change, and leaders (and the church) begin to view success in a new light.

"Whatever it is you celebrate in your culture, that's what people think is the big deal," writes Reggie McNeal in his watershed book, *Missional Renaissance: Changing the Scoreboard for the Church*.[2]

Level 5 churches understand that what you measure improves and what you celebrate gets repeated, so they are careful about what they measure and celebrate. Consider the potential scorecard changes below:

1. Instead of simply asking, "How many people attended church this weekend," a Level 5 church prioritizes, "How many disciples are we making and releasing?"

2. Level 5 churches think about the budget seemingly counter-intuitively, focusing on allocating funds to send leaders and plant new churches.

3. Level 5 churches go beyond measuring small groups to measuring mobilized missions. They quantify how many people are apprentices and how many apprentices are now leading in mission.

4. Level 5 churches measure the number of healthy churches they've multiplied—sometimes at the expense of growing the mother church—and then measure how many churches these new plants have produced. Everyone in the church embraces and embodies the new metric/scoreboard of "go."

Empowering Systems:

1. *A bias to "yes"*: In a Level 5 church, the internal culture creates and affords a bias to "yes." Again, "You can do it; we can help." In other words, Level 5 churches have a permission-giving culture, allowing disciples to plant, grow and reproduce disciples and new churches in incarnational forms that may not look like the prevailing church form.

2. *A sending impulse*: Level 5 multiplying churches create and develop decentralized and empowering systems that grow and release power among the people of the church, empowering *and* equipping disciples so that multiplication

47

spreads spontaneously and exponentially. In Level 5 churches, people don't ask, "Am I called to ministry?" They inherently know they are called to ministry. The only real question is, "What ministry has God called me to?"

In his book, *Saturate*, Soma Communities Founder Jeff Vanderstelt tells numerous stories about how people in the missional community are pursuing their ministry in their local community. In one story, a Soma community adopted a public high school football team in such a sustained, comprehensive way that they asked one of the community's members (who knows little about football) to serve on the committee to select the next football coach, saying, "You don't know football, but you do know character."

"Many Christians have unwittingly embraced the idea that ministry is what pastors do on Sundays rather than the 24/7 calling of all believers," Vanderstelt writes. "God has called His people to something bigger: a view of the Christian life that encompasses the ordinary, the extraordinary and everything in between."[3]

3.   *Easily accessible*: Level 5 churches believe that *everyone* gets to play. They grasp that multiplication must be easy to implement, giving every person in the church the opportunity to engage. Complex content and processes are not easily transferrable or reproduced. Multiplication relies on simple, reproducible strategies that can be easily duplicated and adapted.

4.   *A minimal ecclesiology*: Level 5 churches wrestle with the question, "What is church for us?" However, that tension doesn't mean they water down Scripture in *any* way. A minimal ecclesiology is fundamental to multiplication strategies.

5.   *Messy/insecure/risky*: A Level 5 multiplying church and their leaders realize that creating a culture of multiplication is a

messy, often insecure, and high-risk pursuit. Just like in nature, church multiplication is not an easy, cut-and-dried, prescriptive process devoid of conflict and chaos. Multiplying leaders know it will be chaordic. Creating something new is always challenging as unexpected circumstances and people introduce new tensions. Level 5 churches have a "theology of experimentation," including failure, that says, "God is at work in the midst of this mess."

Adaptive systems: Adaptive systems are 1) emerging—developing from the bottom up, creating space for new and unpredictable forms from the church that created them; 2) self-organizing—with people mutually adjusting their behaviors to cope with changing internal and external environmental demands; and 3) collaborative—ushering in the body of Christ and their gifts to work together to carry out a shared mission. In an adaptive system, church leaders must lead with *missio Dei* in mind. God's mission drives the leadership, which seeks to empower and equip everyone in the church to engage in the common mission. The question is not, "Does the church have a mission?" but instead, "Does the mission have a church?"

Liberated financial systems: Perhaps one of the greatest barriers to Level 5 multiplication is finances, keeping a church dependent on a static system that produces the funds they need to keep going. Level 5 multiplication happens when a church's financial systems allow the church to make the mission of God (multiplying disciples) their No. 1 priority vs. keeping the church financially viable. Liberated financial systems don't get in the way of mission. Instead, they free the church to experiment with new and unconventional ways of doing things (such as bi-vocational leadership and church-operated 501C3 businesses) to accomplish the mission.

Apostolic atmosphere: Level 5 churches embrace the spectrum of APEST that Ephesians 4 gives us. Here in this passage, Paul calls us to unity, writing about the fivefold giftings (apostles, prophets, evangelists, shepherds and teachers). He reminds us that to be a complete expression of the church, we need everyone using their individual gifting. The spectrum of the gifts brings not only unity but also maturity in the faith. Yet the prevailing model of the U.S. Church tends to champion pastors and teachers while pushing aside apostles, prophets and evangelists.

By definition, "apostolic" is characteristic of the 12 apostles—Christ-called leaders who took Christianity to the world. Level 5 churches embrace the spectrum of APEST and recognize that an apostolic atmosphere—focused on sending and releasing—is crucial to Level 5 multiplication. As apostolic leaders provide strategic missional perspective, apostolic influence awakens the church to its true calling. In the words of author Alan Hirsch in *The Forgotten Ways*:

"There is something essential and irreplaceable in the ministry of the apostle that is critical to the emergence of missional movements like that of the biblical and postbiblical periods and of the underground phenomenon of the Chinese church."[4]

Level 5 churches activate apostolic leaders inside the church instead of "exiling" them to leadership in non-profit organizations and para church ministries. For example, The Navigators ministry rose out of a calling to evangelize and disciple people outside the church structures because the church was not effective at it.[5]

A church with an apostolic atmosphere facilitates the expansion of the faith and the church by valuing, experimenting with, and establishing new incarnational expressions and models.

Level 5 leadership: A Level 5 church has humble, tenacious leaders who are continuous "learners"—openhanded leaders whose bias is toward "yes." Humility allows these leaders to champion these new incarnational expressions even when the idea or initiative isn't their own.

At Tampa Bay, Florida-based Underground, the church mobilizes, resources and empowers what they call "micro churches." Led by planter Brian Sanders, the church is a fellowship of 100-plus micro churches, with the larger church expression serving the smaller. Sanders' conviction that *people* make up the church (not buildings, budgets, or leaders) has unleashed an apostolic atmosphere in the church, as the Underground multiplies rapidly through fresh expressions of faith led by individuals or groups—instead of Sanders or other leaders. Typically, these micro churches are not Sanders' or other leaders' ideas or initiatives.

Level 5 leaders will likely be that "paradoxical combination of deep humility and ferocious resolve," Jim Collins describes in his watershed book, *Good to Great*.[6]

We suspect that there may be other Level 5 churches we're not yet aware of because their leaders aren't looking to be found. Level 5 leaders don't rely on large, highly publicized events that attract attention. They measure their impact in subtler yet ultimately more profound ways.

Note: Below, I devote an entire section to the role of Level 5 leadership. Our team believes so strongly in this essential multiplication element that we selected "Becoming a Level 5 Leader" as Exponential's 2018 theme.

Kingdom-centric/geo-centric: Level 5 churches take responsibility for the gospel saturation of a city or geography. They long to see a place so rich with the people and the Kingdom of God that every man, woman and child in their city has a daily encounter with Jesus in word and deed. Focusing on Kingdom multiplication forces them to think outside the framework of their own church to find ways to partner with other churches, denominations, networks, para church ministries, businesses, social organizations, schools, government, the arts and others to create a synergy greater than the sum of their parts.

A Level 5 multiplying church devotes less energy and fewer resources to building their kingdom (their church) and spends more energy and resources on seeing Jesus build God's Kingdom. In his book, *Kingdom Matrix*, Jeff Christopherson, vice president of the North American Mission Board's SEND Network, identifies characteristics of a Kingdom-centric church.

"The Kingdom-centric church holds as its highest value the redemptive mission of God and understands the difference between tools (worship services, buildings, staff) and purpose (becoming a rescuing and restoring community)," Christopherson writes. "Just because a church claims to be a community of Christ does not automatically mean that it is advancing the cause of Christ. The Kingdom of God advances only through the counter-cultural faith steps of allegiance to the King."[7]

A Kingdom-centric church recognizes that a movement of expanding God's Kingdom lies in the heart of every Christ follower and calls each person to see themselves as a movement maker and Kingdom builder. Geo-centric churches dedicate themselves to having Kingdom life touch society and cultural domains by making and multiplying disciples that tend to focus on transforming their city and the world.

Mission Orange County Executive Catalyst Chris Lagerlof comments that a geography-centric church leader first asks, "How's my city doing?" and then, "How's our church doing?" A passion for their city demands that geo-centric churches work prayerfully, collaboratively and strategically to discover how their city works and its unique aspects.

"Sometimes, we get so fixed on the numbers and percentages that we actually miss the whole geography surrounding us," Lagerlof says. "Our focus becomes more about how many kids live in the community as opposed to how we can impact the schools they go to."

Relational affiliation to a tribe, family or network: Leaders of Level 5 multiplying churches and networks understand the importance of community and belonging. The relational connections in Level 5 movements will come as much (or more) from a sense of "tribe" and "family" as they will from shared resources. From a sense of shared value and mission, affiliations will be voluntary, enabling the church to be as small as necessary to reach every nook and cranny while at the same time large enough to make a huge collective impact.

Everyone is a missionary: In a sense, this characteristic isn't separate from the nine others above. You can see it woven throughout nearly all of them. But this value is worth its own category because it is foundational to a Level 5 church. If there is to be a movement of God in the West, He will do it—one way or the other—with everyday Christ followers.

Dr. Charles Spurgeon is generally credited with the familiar quote: "Every Christian is either a missionary or an imposter." Yet much of what we do in the prevailing model of church works against empowering the priesthood of all believers (1 Peter 2:4-10). Too often, we water down what if means to be a Christ follower. We remove the adventure and the risk, giving people a weak, emaciated view of a relationship with God that only demands attendance on three out of four Sundays, 2 percent of our income, and a mission project once or twice a year.

When we continue to dumb down what it means to be a disciple of Jesus, we stifle the Church. A Level 5 church does not seek to demote the clergy but rather to promote the laity. Imagine what would happen if just 10 percent of the people that attend weekend services truly embraced the fact that they're a full-time missionary/pastor.

Level 5 churches know how to help people understand their primary calling while proactively developing systems and processes to help individuals find their unique, personal calling. In Level 5 churches, believers understand who they are called to be, what they are called to do, and where they are called to go.

Wade Burnett, a lawyer, church planter and consultant at Multisite Solutions, is part of our national Becoming Five team. After our November 2016 gathering, Wade said the following:

"We are using the [characteristics] as the foundation for our new church. All of our ministries (including the weekend services) will be organized around the following foundations that we will teach continually in all contexts:

1) Jesus is Lord
2) The Kingdom of God is here (Kingdom-centric).
3) The King has given us a mission (disciple making).
4) We all play (Ephesians 4).
5) We all embrace change (life transformation//adaptive systems).
6) We all reproduce (apostolic impulse//multiplication).

Wade continued, "I wanted you to know about this new church, but more than that I wanted to share the immediate impact this framework is having on our new congregation. Praying the Lord will do with it what only He can."

The road ahead for Wade and this new church will not be easy. But they are courageously stepping out in faith to shift their paradigm and the prevailing addition-focused scorecard. As a growing number of leaders follow this path, imagine the impact—moving the needle from less than 4 percent of churches ever reproducing to greater than 10 percent.

Note: Before moving on to chapter 4, I strongly encourage you to work through the Perspective questions and rate yourself on each of these 10 characteristics using chapter 3 in the Dream Big Workbook. *Then work through them with your team to gain shared perspective.*

Chapter 4
Paradigm
What Must Change?

"Put off your old self, which is being corrupted by its deceitful
desires; to be made new in the attitude of your minds; and to
put on the new self" (Eph. 4:22-24).

Creating a culture of multiplication around the 10 characteristics of
Level 5 churches requires a shift in our paradigm. We need new
wineskins and new thinking. The national team of leaders
collaborating to identify these characteristics has identified five
key shifts in our paradigm that are essential to creating a culture of
multiplication.

These shifts, as articulated by discipleship author and speaker
Dave Rhodes, include:

1.   **A shift in the hero story for the primary leader**...*from
being the hero to becoming the mentor who creates heroes that
become mentors.*

Becoming a Level 5 church starts with the pursuit of becoming
a Level 5 leader. Every true shift in a church or organization
begins with a personal or heart change in the primary leader.
Story after story tells us that leaders who want to see change
organizationally but don't take the time to make the necessary
personal shifts will rarely experience the results they desire.
Marked by a sense of holy and humble tenacity, the Level 5
leader shifts from being simply the hero of the church and
instead uses his/her power and influence in a mentoring role to
help others become the heroes and the future mentors the
church will need.

2.   **A shift in expectation for every believer**...*from being
consumers or converts to being disciples who make disciples
who make disciples to the fourth generation.*

55

Discipleship is the core of healthy Kingdom multiplication. To shift from being a community of consumers coming each week to gain their spiritual fix, the Level 5 church trains their people in the character and competency of Jesus, empowering and equipping them to make disciples who make disciples to the fourth generation. This means that Level 5 churches start asking future questions: How many fourth-generation disciples does our church have? Have we seen that number increase from last year to this year? Is what we're doing now going to get us to the fourth generation?

3. **A shift in opportunity for every disciple**...*from being a volunteer in a church to becoming a missionary to a mission field waiting to be declared.*

This distinctive may be the most important of any of the shifts. Level 5 churches take the priesthood of believers seriously. To become disciples who make disciples who make disciples, people must start thinking of themselves differently—as potential pastors or missionaries with a church waiting to be birthed among those with whom they live, work and play.

4. **A shift in operation for the system**...*from the bias of "no" to the bias of "yes."*

Becoming a Level 5 church means shifting the systems of the church, being open to redefining what a church actually is, and then helping people learn to live with the sense of permission that's already inside of them. Uncovering this inherent permission allows us to step into everything God has called us to be and do.

When we shift the operation system, we redesign our systems to move from, "We can do it; you can help," to what should now be a familiar concept: "You can do it; we can help." We develop adaptive and empowering systems that change and shift quickly to move from high command and control at the center, to creating a culture at the edges that quickly and easily says "yes." By clearly defining our core mission (making disciples), we can decentralize, allowing our church to adapt and multiply into new contexts without spending unnecessary time on bureaucratic decision-making.

5. **A shift in the scorecard**...*from counting the number of people in any one church to the percentage of a population changed. From accumulation to transformation.*

Level 5 churches measure success differently than other churches. Instead of just counting the number of people who come to the church, Level 5 churches are more concerned with the growth of the Kingdom among their surrounding neighborhoods and networks. Functioning from a collaborative Kingdom mindset, this means creating change within a population distinctive that's bigger than what any one church could do on its own. This shift requires us to create networks or families of churches that work together to see the "win."

The Role of Level 5 Multiplication Leaders

As we look ahead, we're pressing into understanding the vital role of the Level 5 leader in leading essential paradigm shifts. Level 5 churches must be led by Level 5 leaders who are passionate about creating and maintaining a biblical culture of multiplication. So far, we've identified several integrated areas that shape a Level 5 multiplication leader. Level 5 leaders should:

1. Understand, own, and manage the three dimensions of healthy multiplication: disciple making, capacity building, and empowering systems for mobilization.

2. Understand, own, and manage the 10 characteristics of a Level 5 culture (described in chapter 3).

3.   Understand, own, and manage the above five paradigm shifts required for creating Level 5 culture (discussed above).

4.   Have the courage to surrender their egocentric scorecards and embrace a multiplication scorecard.

5.   Do the hard work of getting perspective, creating a vision for multiplication, and developing a plan for the future.

Pause and Reflect

Feeling a bit overwhelmed? Don't worry! It's natural. Finding perspective is actually the most painful part of the process. It requires us to face the brutal facts of our present reality, to surrender our current weaknesses more fully to God, and to seek His provision for a better future.

Before moving forward, you may want to encourage each of your team members to work through this chapter and then spend time together reflecting, praying and working through the Perspective questions in chapter 4 of the *Dream Big Workbook.*

Consider leading a staff retreat to process and work toward a common, shared perspective using the workbook exercises from chapters 2 through 4. The clarity and insights you gain about your past and present culture from these perspective chapters will give you a solid foundation for developing a vision and strategy in the coming chapters.

Ultimately, the best pathway to a shared, common vision is through a shared, common perspective. Taking the necessary time to prepare will create the solid foundation essential to moving forward in defining a pathway to a new multiplication vision for you and your church.

Chapter 5
Pursuit
Where Do We Want to Go?

"Now glory be to God, who by his mighty power at work within us is able to do far more than we would ever dare to ask or even dream of—infinitely beyond our highest prayers, desires, thoughts, or hopes"
(Ephesians 3:20, TLB).

I love what Paul says here in his letter to the church at Ephesus. God has big dreams for us—"infinitely beyond" anything we can fathom. What does that look like for you and your church?

To answer this question, we had to start with another question: Why do we exist? As we learned in chapter 2, our core purpose is making disciples that make disciples. It is why the Church exists. Jesus commanded it, leaving no wiggle room for man-made diversions.

In this chapter, we're building on that foundation and the perspective we gained in chapters 2 through 4 to look at the question, "Where do we want to go or who do we want to become?" This question is rooted in our God-given dreams, manifested in a vision for our church.

Go back to the puzzle analogy we discussed in chapter 1. Like the picture on the box, our vision communicates a clear and compelling image of the future. It's something to move toward and pursue. Vision is often futuristic, vivid, compelling and seemingly beyond the efforts of human hands. It requires us to rely on God to deliver something more than we can physically see. In practical terms, vision gives context to where we're going. It's a commitment to who we want to become.

How strongly is your vision rooted in planting churches that plant churches?

A vision rooted in multiplication conveys a strong commitment to sending and releasing disciples to plant churches that plant churches. When our vision is greater than growing and expanding our kingdom, the fruit of disciple making produces churches that plant churches—ultimately growing and expanding God's Kingdom.

The Paradox of Vision

For church leaders, vision provides a bit of a paradox. On one hand, we know through Scripture that God will hold us accountable for being good stewards of the resources He entrusts to our care. We all want to face Jesus some day and hear Him say, "Well done, good and faithful servant." Like the servants in the parable of the talents, we must act to risk and extend the resources the Master gives us. Vision stretches us to be fruitful.

On the other hand, we know that God cares more about our faithfulness and surrender to Him and His plans than our man-made visions and strategies.

Consider the pursuits of Noah, Abraham, Peter, Paul, Nehemiah and Ruth. Were their visions clear and world- changing? Not at all. These leaders we look to didn't know what they were doing. Noah couldn't comprehend God's bigger picture. Abraham said "yes" and didn't even know where he was going. Peter and Paul had no human idea how God would use them in the greatest movement in history. Nehemiah simply wanted to rebuild some walls and had no idea of God's bigger vision to rescue His people. And Ruth, she died without knowing the real legacy she'd leave in Jesus' lineage.

The heroes of the faith were known more for their faithfulness to cooperate with and surrender to God than they were their vision or strategy. When Jesus shared the last supper with His disciples and prayed for them, He could have laid out the master plan and grand vision for a world movement. Instead, He prayed for their faithfulness and after His resurrection, gave them His Great Commission (Matt. 28:19).

We get in trouble not for our lack of vision, but for our lack of obedience to "go" rather than "stay," and "accumulate" rather than "send"—making cultural Christians instead of biblical disciples. When our vision is more about living *our* dreams than God's dreams and building *our* strategies rather than cooperating in His plans, our good intentions for multiplication will always fail.

Granted, God's ways are often counter-intuitive to our ways. Would you ever strategize to conquer a city by marching around its walls and blowing trumpets? Or rescue a group of people from the bondage of slavery using the tongue of a man with a self-professed speech problem? Or repopulate the world through a man who spent 100 years building a giant boat with no blueprints? Or save the world from sin through the birth of a baby born of a virgin girl? His ways are definitely not our ways.

Your key question is not, "Where do *we* want to go?" or "Who do *we* want to become?" but rather, "Where does *God* want our church to go?" and, "Who does *He* want us to become?" In his classic study, *Experiencing God,* author Henry Blackaby perfectly summarizes the approach we need to take in developing vision in this familiar statement: "Watch to see where God is working and join Him."[1] Perhaps a lesser-known Blackaby insight comes from his book, *Spiritual Leadership: Moving People on to God's Agenda.* Obedience, he says, is key.

"If Christians around the world were to suddenly renounce their personal agendas, their life goals and their aspirations, and begin responding in radical obedience to everything God showed them, the world would be turned upside down," Blackaby writes. "How do we know? Because that's what first-century Christians did, and the world is still talking about it."[2]

We need to discover God's dream and vision, and then build our dreams around His. Too many times, we do the reverse. Yes, you need a unique vision for where God wants to take you and your church—the destination on the GPS. You also need strategy for getting there. But God must be the source of both.

We all need big dreams to keep us moving when the challenges come and spur us on to far more we would ever dare to ask or imagine—infinitely beyond our prayers, desires, thoughts or hopes.

Permission to Dream Big

Have you ever thought that big dreams are the birthright of every believer? Throughout Scripture, the most basic words of our faith—hope, promise, Heaven, eternity—connect us to our future. Scripture is filled with verses that urge us to look forward. To follow God is to find strange confidence that "He rewards those who seek Him," even in challenging circumstances. Faith makes us future-people.

For leaders, big dreams are often our starting point. At some place in your life, God found you again. You were already saved, but a new idea struck you and stuck with you. Look at some of the big dreams today's multiplication leaders are pursuing:

1.   About a decade ago, The Summit Church sensed God giving them what Planter/Pastor J.D. Greear calls "an audacious vision" of planting 1,000 churches by the year 2050—three times as many churches as attendees in the Raleigh, North Carolina, congregation. Starting with only two missionary families in the field, The Summit Church continues to make notable progress and press on toward their dream, Greear says—all while praying "God-sized prayers."

2.   When New Life Church was three years old, the leadership team made a fundamental decision to be a church that focused on Kingdom growth over its own growth. That one decision has shaped the DNA of the Chantilly, Virginia, church. In 2004, New Life began to dream of moving from one church plant every four years to one per year. Now, the church is

pursuing an aggressive multiplication vision of planting 20 churches each year.

3.   In November 2016, the Evangelical Free Church of America (EFCA) began to wrestle with the challenge of moving toward a sustained 10 percent rate of multiplication. For EFCA, that means one out of every 10 EFCA churches will start a new church or campus each year, tripling the number of church plants. Currently (in early 2017), the denomination averages 2.5 percent to 3 percent of churches multiplying each year. "That [increase] is a huge number," said Jeff Sorvik, EFCA Church Multiplication Catalyst. "God-sized changes require God's power."[3]

4.   In 2009, The Austin Stone launched the 100 People Network, a long-term initiative that engages the entire congregation in three roles (goers, senders and front-end mobilizers) to send 100 people from the church for two years or more to reach the 6,000 unreached people groups in the world.

"From the very beginning we've really defined our success by not how many people we could get through the doors but by how many people we can equip and send out," says Lead Pastor Matt Carter. "The heart of that is the Great Commission. We asked, 'What can we do in this limited amount of time that God has given us to make a dent in the Great Commission?'"[4]

Jesus' Multiplication Dream

The dream God gives each of us exists as part of a bigger dream rooted in Scripture. Right before His ascension into Heaven, Jesus shared His dream for His Church—His vision for multiplication:

"You will receive power when the Holy Spirit comes up on you; and you will be my witnesses in Jerusalem, and in all Judea and Samaria, and to the ends of the earth" (Acts 1:8).

The dream that Jesus gave His present and future followers focused on a movement. He had a powerful vision of God's Kingdom coming on earth as it is in heaven. Through the Holy Spirit, we have the power to venture beyond our home base and ultimately take His Good News to every tribe and every nation so that one day, "at the name of Jesus every knee should bow ... and every tongue confess that Jesus Christ is Lord" (Phil. 2:10-11).

Jesus knew that gargantuan dream would not be accomplished with one or even 1 million churches. As Christ followers and leaders of His church, He is asking us to dream big with Him to accomplish His mission and grow His Kingdom. In the process, He grows and matures us. If you don't already know it, dreaming big is a true life-changer.

Allowing your heart and mind to pursue a vision that's bigger than you will change you in significant ways. When we begin to get a clear vision for multiplication both as a leader and for our church, we start to see how God prepares and shapes us for that vision.

Dreaming Big Changes Your Questions

When it comes to big dreams, one question will lead to another. The size of your dream will often determine the types of questions you ask. Easily manageable smaller dreams require one set of questions while big dreams will lead you to ask an entirely different set of questions. Since starting NewThing Network, Dave Ferguson's questions have changed with the size of his dreams.

"Ten years ago, our dream was to start a network of new churches, so I had to ask, *How can I attract, train and deploy church planters?* Now our dream is to see a movement of reproducing churches, so I'm asking, *How can I create systems that reproduce networks and attract, train and deploy apostolic leaders?"*

As you start to ask the challenging questions that will help lead you toward your multiplication vision, your scorecard for how you measure success will begin to change. In chapter 3, we said that

64

one of the 10 characteristics of Level 5 multiplying churches is their adoption of a new scoreboard. While we may still ask, "How many people worshipped with us this weekend," a multiplication vision requires us to think toward the future and identify new metrics of success:

1. How many churches will we plant this year and over the next five years?
2. Will we budget significantly for church multiplication (an actual line item)?
3. How many new churches outside our own church will we support?
4. Will we release and send out leaders to multiply churches—even the most valuable ones?
5. How many people will we encourage to leave and start a new church?
6. If we pursue multiplication and our weekend attendance goes down as a result, will we see ourselves as successful?

Your vision should represent how you want to measure the future success of your church as well as your personal success. The greater your multiplication vision, the more profound the questions you will ask and the more your scorecard will change.

Dreaming Big Changes Your Prayers

Big dreams drive us to our knees. A vision for multiplication that's too big for you and your church to accomplish through your own efforts and giftings keeps you looking to God and depending on Him.

For West Ridge Church Planter/Pastor Brian Bloye, prayer was a catalyst to the church's transformation from a congregation focused on size and growth into a community bent on Kingdom multiplication.

"I knew that God was going to have to do a work in our staff, and in the leadership of our church," Bloye explains. "And then He was going to have to do a work in our church. Even though I knew it would be a hard work, I knew that if I was praying about multiplication, if I was praying about reproduction, if I was praying about sending, then I was praying in line with God's will. If you pray in line with God's will, you will begin to pray powerful prayers."

As Exponential has directed its focus, energy and resources to Kingdom multiplication, the prayers of Exponential Co-Founder Dave Ferguson have changed. Each day in his journal, he writes "4% > 10%."

"Every day I pray, 'God, use Exponential to see the number of multiplying churches in the U.S. go from 4 percent to 10 percent' and then 'God, use NewThing to create a global movement of 10,000 multiplying churches.'"

Big dreams cause us to pray persistently. Any journey we take toward multiplication will be plagued with internal and external tensions. As we pray persistently and fervently, asking God to search our hearts (internal) and guide us through adversity (external), these tensions drive us closer to God.

In his free eBook, *Flow: Unleashing a River of Multiplication in Your Church, City and World*, Larry Walkemeyer, pastor of Light & Life Fellowship in Long Beach, California, shares how confronting his internal tensions through prayer began to deepen his relationship with God. The more often and honestly he prayed, the more God showed him how his heart needed to change before he could move his church toward a culture of multiplication.

"I had to do a tough and candid assessment of the scorecard that was motivating me to produce results," Walkemeyer says. "God had to do a work *in* me before He could do a work *through* me. During that process, He revealed several things that needed to change in me to enable the changes that were needed in my church."[5]

Dreaming Big Changes Others

Big dreams are contagious. Imagine for a minute the impact of the dreams on another and how they influenced history:

1. How did Abraham's faith open the door for Isaac's walk with God?
2. Would Joshua have conquered Canaan without the life lessons of his mentor, Moses?
3. How did Ruth's mother-in-law prepare her to be the great-grandmother to a king?
4. Where would God's people be today if Mordecai had never challenged Esther?
5. Where would Paul be had Barnabas not taken a risk on him?
6. Without Paul's involvement in his life, would Timothy have gone on to lead?

When we get a vision for multiplication and begin to share it, we start a chain reaction. Have you ever seen someone's soul awaken as he/she begins to wonder about the role he/she could play in advancing the Kingdom? Think about whose Kingdom vision has influenced you and made you say, "I want to lead a church that follows the biblical call to multiply disciples." In the same way, your multiplication vision could actually be the match that starts a wildfire! Sharing a clear vision for multiplication will slowly begin to change the people in your path in several ways:

People start to take ownership of the vision. Following a big-dream leader removes much of the mystery about how to pursue a vision. Think for a moment about how the process of visionary leadership is multiplied and transferred as the lead visionary mentors key team players.

Will Mancini has served as a vision architect for hundreds of churches. We partnered with him to help us do what he does best. For more than a decade, Mancini has come alongside teams to help them bring clarity to their vision. Mancini can look back and see how his mentors' big dreams have led him to where he is today.

"I remember serving on Bruce Wesley's leadership team at Clear Creek Community Church in Houston," Mancini says. "I learned a ton about decision-making, communication, integrity and self-discipline. Most importantly, I learned from Bruce's mastery of calling others to commitment. Without his model in my life, I never could have imagined transitioning to a coaching ministry."

Watching a leader achieve his/her dreams removes fear and insecurity for everyone else that might dare to dream. We all know church leaders that relegate visionary leadership to a select few. Scripture tells us that daring to imagine big things is the opportunity of every believer. *People begin to see themselves as visionaries.* Level 5 churches recognize that everyone is part of the vision and that everyone has a unique calling.

I (Will) recall how a lay leader in a church I worked with began to spark a vision in other lay leaders. I watched Tony, a successful lay leader and owner of an electrical supply store, practice leading the new member Starting Point class in his church. He shared how the church had helped him use his business as a platform for the gospel.

As Tony talked, I could see the spark in the eyes of other lay leaders around the room who were helping with his practice exercise. They were catching a bit of his dream, seeing how doable it is to reach others in the daily realities of the job.

Unfortunately, many church leaders don't empower lay leaders to play this kind of role. Instead, they are the "ball hogs" of the Kingdom, never allowing the fruit of Ephesians 4 to grow and mature. Paul tells us that God gives gifted men and woman to the

Church to equip the saints for the work of ministry—not to excuse the saints from the work of ministry.

When you start to dream big about a church that prioritizes Kingdom growth over growing the church, that vision will change others—from the high capacity donor to the risk-taking lay leader, to the high school freshman in your student ministry. If you're aspiring to Level 5 multiplication, the key question is, "How are you preparing for and expecting the chain reaction of visionary leadership to take place and grow?"

Dreaming Big Changes You

Leaders that are pursuing Level 5 multiplication can easily look back to see how dreaming big has changed them personally.

Currently, Dave Ferguson dreams of seeing his Chicago-based church move from Level 4 to Level 5 multiplication. That dream, he says, has transformed him: "Other than becoming a Christ-follower, making the decision to become a multiplying church and pursuing a multiplication vision has been the biggest change in my life as a church leader."

Below, Ferguson identifies the various ways his dream has changed him and other multiplying leaders:

A multiplication vision deepens your relationship with God. Think about how the vision that God gave Moses began to change not only him, but also his relationship with the God who called him out of the desert and into new life. At the crossroads of each and every challenge, Moses' respect for God and His word grew. His trust in God's promises for a future land strengthened him in adversity. Throughout Exodus, we see how Moses' utter dependence on his God for every provision changed him.

When you depend on God to fulfill a vision He has given you, your relationship with God—how you see and respond to Him—changes and changes you.

69

A multiplication vision shapes your closest relationships in ministry. Few people in Scripture exhibit such a noticeable focus on relationships like Paul does. Letter after letter shows us how Paul built relationships with the churches he started. Moreover, the Barnabas > Paul > Timothy powerhouse is one of our strongest examples of mentoring in Scripture. Paul knew his relationships were vital to advancing the gospel. When we pursue a God-given vision, like-minded people with the same passions and goals inevitably cross our paths. Our opportunities to influence and be influenced by high-capacity leaders increase, and we begin to seek out and spend time with people who have our heart for movement and Kingdom focus. Your relationships will change you.

A multiplication vision shapes your priorities. Having a vision keeps us laser-focused. When opportunities come our way with no clear connection to multiplication, it's an easy "no." A clear vision provides us with a filter through which we can run every idea, opportunity and decision. Vision gives you a picture of an unrealized future and the guardrails you need to stay on the path.

Dreaming Big Changes Your Church

How can a clear vision for multiplication change your church? Leaders of multiplying churches can tell story after story of how they've seen their church transform as a result of their focus on a big dream beyond their backyard, city and state.

Casting a clear, compelling vision that calls your church to a specific purpose and mobilizes people into a life of mission lays the foundation for a church that thinks, acts and prays differently than a church focused only on its own growth. A church that carries out a strong multiplication vision begins to develop the characteristics of Level 5 multiplying churches. Consider some of the specific ways a multiplication vision changes your church:

Vision incubates a Kingdom-centric church. When people know and truly grasp that they are part of something bigger than themselves—something with eternal impact—they begin to be less focused on building their kingdom (their church) and more focused on seeing Jesus build God's Kingdom. That means fewer external tensions to navigate and more buy-in on all fronts as you pursue multiplication.

Vision nurtures a culture/community of biblical disciple making. In a church that embraces a vision for multiplication, making and multiplying disciples is paramount. Everyone in the church is a biblical disciple maker, reproducing disciples in community.

In 2016, Celebrate Community Church in Sioux Falls, South Dakota, announced its vision for becoming a Level 5 multiplication church. Lead Pastor Keith Loy is pursuing a vision of raising up disciples within the church to become church planters who will plant 50 churches in 10 years. The church brought 12 potential planters to Exponential East 2016. This Level 5 vision, says Reed DeVries who serves as the "architect" for it, has "transformed the church." Celebrate has asked a local seminary to bring training to their lay people as they plant.

"We caught the vision of Level 5," DeVries says, "and we're not going back."

Vision breeds an apostolic atmosphere. As a leader, your vision for multiplication must be tied to the spectrum of APEST (Ephesians 4), which brings not only unity but also maturity in the faith. Alan Hirsch points to the connection between APEST and a church's "sending" impulse: "When leaders begin to embrace all five giftings of the Church—apostles, prophets, evangelists, shepherds and teachers—the key value of sending and releasing becomes a natural and expected part of your church."

Vision activates your church's "sending" impulse. In a church that has a strong multiplication vision, multiplication spreads spontaneously and exponentially. People know they are called to make disciples. They know that they're part of a church that releases and sends them out to carry the gospel to every nook and cranny of society.

What would it look like if your church embraced and reflected all of these values? How would things be different? How would your community transform? What would it look like for you to lead a church that's sold out to multiplication, working together for the purpose of advancing the Kingdom?

Pursuing a multiplication vision moves us toward this picture.

A Clear Path to a Lesser Goal

So if having a vision for multiplication is such a game-changer in our lives and in our church, what keeps us from dreaming big and following through on those dreams? Let's look at two of the biggest culprits.

1. *Big dreams get buried under the tensions of multiplication.* Despite what we read in Scripture and despite how we spring into ministry, the external tensions of multiplication that we identified in *Spark* and *Becoming a Level 5 Multiplying Church* become reality:

- The leadership team can't understand why you want to give resources to a church planter when the church doesn't even have a building.
- The idea of planting when your church still has unfilled seats seems counter-intuitive.
- People continue to ask, "Why would we send out one of our best leaders to plant another church when our attendance is just starting to increase?"

Other related things shoot down our dreams. For some, it may be burnout. For others, it may be a series of false starts or failures. Have you found yourself running on a ministry treadmill only to wonder what direction you were really headed?

2. *Big dreams get replaced with lesser visions.* Imagine getting a group of venture capitalists fired up about a new restaurant concept that's going be the next phenomenon across the dining landscape of America. As the drum roll begins, you enthusiastically announce, "We are going to serve food!"

I (Will) call this "generic vision"—vision that's bland and nondescript. Generic vision doesn't change anybody or anything. Despite the fact that most leaders in ministry are truly visionaries, they fall prey to generic forms of ministry vision all of the time. How many times have you heard a church say its vision is to "to reach more people for Christ," or "to change the world?"

Although many leaders start out with a big dream for multiplication, that dream is difficult to keep alive. But it really doesn't go away completely as much as it drifts toward generic kinds of vision. At that point, we miss the opportunity to engage people in a specific dream.

Think about this statement: "We are kept from our goal not by obstacles but by a clear path to a lesser goal." When you lead with generic vision, you're leading toward a lesser goal. It's not the real dream that God has for you and your church. It doesn't possess any of the impact a clear vision is supposed to have. Proverbs 28:19 tells us, "When people can't see what God is up to, they stumble all over themselves" (*The Message*).

Think of generic vision another way: It's actually robbing you of progress. You won't even get close to realizing your church's full multiplication potential with a generic sense of your church's future. I like what pastor and best-selling author Rick Warren says about vision: A vision is only dynamic when it's specific. You need a specific and actionable vision.

In my book, *God Dreams*, I share a list of the different kinds of generic vision. Each type is rooted in healthy biases. As I studied generic vision, it struck me that we drift toward generic because of healthy biases. While good leadership is the basis for these biases,

73

they lead to generic vision if taken too far."[6]

In chapter 5 of the *Dream Big Workbook*, I identify and describe the three types of biases that propel us toward generic vision: a bias for biblical accuracy, a bias for growth, and a bias for efficiency. The workbook also includes reflection questions to help you assess if you're avoiding generic vision.

Moving Forward: Defining Your Vision

In chapter 5 of the *Dream Big Workbook*, I offer several Vision Exercises to help you and your team define and refine your church's big dream for multiplication. Use these exercises to prompt and guide your vision process.

Our hope is that these Vision Exercises will help you lead your team to start to uncover the unique multiplication dream for your church. How you get there—your strategy—might shift or change over time. But a clear vision for multiplication is essential to every church leader aspiring to become a Level 5 multiplying church.

God never wants you to stop dreaming. You should always have a vision for multiplying your church. Remember that it's not *your* vision. Whatever we pursue should be God's vision. As I said at the beginning of this chapter, Jesus' dream is about a movement— to make disciples "to the ends of the earth." In the next chapter, Todd shares the specific pathways you can take to get you to your unique multiplication dream.

Chapter 6
Pathways
What Can We Expect?

"Give careful thought to the paths for your
feet and be steadfast in all your ways (Proverbs 4:26).

"Two roads diverged in a wood and I -
I took the one less traveled by,
and that has made all the difference."[1]
~ Robert Frost

How many times has your smart phone come to the rescue?
Because I travel quite a bit, I'm constantly relying on my phone to
get me to where I need to go. Using specific data (my destination
and current location), my phone's GPS maps a course for me.
Often, the GPS will give me several pathway options. For
example, I live in the suburbs of Washington, D.C. From my house
to the city, I can take three different primary pathways.

To identify the different pathways, the GPS considers numerous
factors including distance, time, traffic, accidents, and toll roads.
At any given time, the GPS uses the unique combination of these
factors to identify the best pathway. And if traffic is heavy or some
other obstacle comes up, the GPS continues to make route
adjustments even after I choose a primary route and start driving.
In fact, often the actual pathway I use is different than the initial
one.

Our journey toward multiplication is surprisingly similar. When
we gain perspective and understand where we currently are as a
church (chapters 3 and 4), and then discern a vision for where we'd
like to go in the future (chapter 5), a pathway for the journey
emerges.

A pathway is a route or way of access to a destination; a way of reaching or achieving something.[2] It connects our current reality to a more desirable future. Moving toward a future of Level 5 multiplication offers several primary pathways common to most churches. By understanding these pathways, you can learn what to expect on your multiplication journey. Throughout this chapter, we're looking at the most common and primary pathways to Level 5 multiplication.

The Big Picture: Your Starting Point and Destination

If you've completed the free online Becoming Five assessment and worked through the exercises in the *Dream Big Workbook*, you already have a pretty clear idea of your starting point and your desired destination. The assessment gives you a score (Level 1-5) and a pattern representing your past, present and future. A pattern simply gives you a snapshot of where your church has been, where you are, and where you'd like to go. For example, if your pattern is 2-3-4, you were a Level 2 church in the past, a Level 3 church today, and you aspire to be a Level 4 church in the future. The "3-4" numbers (your current level of multiplication and your future aspiration for multiplication) indicate your pathway. We'd say your pathway is from "3 to 4."

If you're a new church, the assessment gives you a score (1-5) reflecting your aspirational level of multiplication. Because you're new, you don't have history to establish a pattern. You'll score something like "0-0-5." This means you're a new church, and you aspire to become Level 5. Your pathway is "New to 5."

If you've taken the assessment, write your numerical pattern and descriptive pathway below (for example, "3 to 4," or "New to 5," etc.). If you've not yet taken the free assessment at becomingfive.org, let me strongly encourage you to stop now and complete it before you continue. It takes less than 30 minutes to finish, and results are available immediately.

My Numerical Pattern (e.g., 2-3-4):

My Descriptive Pathway (e.g. "3 to 4"):

From Pattern to Pathway

The assessment offers 125 possible different numerical patterns between 1-1-1 and 5-5-5. In *Becoming a Level Five Multiplying Church*, I explained that we could condense these 125 patterns down to seven primary ones. As you carefully look at the differences in each of the seven patterns, you'll see unique challenges and issues for each one:

 Aspiring pattern - These churches are at Level 1 and 2, but they aspire to move to Levels 4 and 5. Churches in this pattern must first internalize the value of multiplication before they can transform their behaviors.

 Advancing pattern - These churches have moved from Level 1 or 2 to Level 3, and now seek to move to Level 4 or 5. They are aggressively advancing and now must overcome the strong tensions in Level 3 that can keep them in an addition-growth culture.

 Breakout pattern - These churches are stuck (or happy) at Level 3. They now seek to break out to Level 4 or 5, but they must first overcome the strong restraining tension at Level 3.

 Reproducing pattern - These churches have already moved from Level 3 to Level 4. They continue to feel the tensions at Level 3, yet they strongly want to continue increasing to Level 5 multiplication.

 Recovery pattern – These churches have decreased from past to present and then increased to an aspirational score of 4 or 5—for example, a 3-2-4. Recovery pattern churches have experienced growth in their history followed by some difficulties.

 Addition pattern - Churches with an addition pattern have a strong addition-growth scorecard at Level 3. Possibly caught in the grip of addition culture, they have not yet embraced a future aspiration for multiplication.

Survivor pattern – The "future" score of churches with this pattern points to Level 2. These churches may be struggling and have difficulty seeing beyond survival thinking, thus the low score on their aspirations.

Churches with Addition or Survivor patterns are just flat out not aspiring to Levels 4 and 5. They are either stuck or happy with their current level of multiplication. To move toward multiplication, these churches must first undergo a transformation in their values and vision to establish a sincere desire for multiplication. If that kind of revolutionary shift happens, the multiplication pattern will change to reflect one of the other five patterns. If not, they will remain stuck at their current levels.

The other patterns for existing churches, plus the "0-0-4" and "0-0-5" patterns for new churches, represent the core patterns for multiplication. We can express these patterns as one of six different "pathways" to multiplication. The six pathways to multiplication include:

Core pathways

Level 3 to 4
Level 4 to 4+
New to 4
New to 5
Level 1 or 2 to 4

Derivative pathways - These pathways either "derive" or find their context using specific elements of the core pathways; or they are pathways we have yet to fully understand and discover:

Levels 1, 2, 3, or 4 to 5

Over the next few pages, I describe each of these pathways, including key characteristics and tensions. My hope is you'll come away from these sections with a clear understanding of each pathway and the insight you'll need to follow it toward multiplication.

The Elephant in the Room

If you've paid close attention to the last section, you may be asking, "Where are the core pathways for existing churches to Level 5?" We've highlighted only one core pathway to Level 5— via new churches. This exclusion grows out of several hard questions our national team has wrestled with:

1. Is it really possible for an existing church to break free from the strong grip of the Level 3 magnet to become a Level 5 church?
2. Can the prevailing operating system that grows a church to Level 3 evolve into a system that produces Level 5 multiplication? Or must the old operating system be replaced with an entirely new one?
3. With less than 0.1 percent of U.S. churches at Level 5, is our current paradigm of church even capable of producing a movement of Level 5 churches?

These and other similar questions have burdened the national team of leaders working on the multiplication content in this book. In chapter 1 of *Becoming a Level Five Multiplying Church*, I addressed the need for us to rethink our current operating system.

"We believe that the strengths of this current operating system—attracting and connecting with people far from

79

God—are essential and to be celebrated. But we're deeply convicted that the prevailing operating system new church planters so passionately embrace also has shortcomings in producing the transformation needed to both fuel and sustain multiplication movements. The current system is perfectly aligned to give us accumulation and addition growth.

"We stand at a crossroads in history with the opportunity to pilot a better future. But to make this revolutionary change, we need to rethink our current operating systems and become courageous leaders willing to discover and embrace new ones."[3]

It appears the journey to Level 5 requires revolutionary change—not simply evolutionary progression. While we're uncertain if existing churches can make the radical, revolutionary changes necessary in their operating systems to become Level 5, we are certain of these things:

1. New churches that are unconstrained by old wineskins and willing to lead revolutionary change can become Level 5.
2. Existing churches can programmatically become Level 4, and even 4+ (aggressive and vibrant version of Level 4) churches.
3. Level 3 churches represent a strong and significant resource base and influence in the U.S. church. Seeing these churches embrace a new and better scorecard via the journey to Level 4 is a game changer. Every 1 percent increase in churches at Level 4 represents huge Kingdom impact. We need to see Level 4 become the new normal in churches. Level 3 churches are the best place to start.
4. Level 4 churches are perfectly positioned to coach and mentor the next generation of church planters on the pathway to Level 5.
5. Level 4 churches are resourced and positioned to become incubators and research and development (R&D) platforms for experimenting with new operating systems for Level 5

multiplication. These churches can champion Level 5 activities, however they'll need to unbridle them from the prevailing structures and controls. These churches will need to be true R&D projects with significant freedom, flexibility and autonomy to experiment (and even fail).

Exponential's *big dream* is to see the percentage of churches at Levels 4 and 5 move from less than 4 percent to greater than 10 percent in our generation!

A Deeper Look Into the Core Pathways

Based on your online multiplication assessment results, what is your pathway to multiplication? Again, the last two numbers of your multiplication pattern indicate your specific pathway. Use the following descriptions to better understand the journey to multiplication for your pathway. You may want to leverage this clarity to refine and adjust your multiplication vision.

Level 3 to 4

Level 3 characteristics: Level 3 churches make up approximately 16 percent of all U.S. churches. For these churches, the scorecard is rooted in addition growth and accumulation. Level 3 churches build their budgets around key growth drivers, including buildings, staff, programs, outreach, marketing, etc. They find it difficult to release and send out their best staff and volunteers to plant churches.

These churches tend to be programmatic with centralized control and decision-making processes. They know how to add (or reproduce) worship services and may have reproduced sites or locations as part of their growth strategy. They have a history of conquering the next growth barrier. As they consider moving to Level 4, these churches often feel *significant* tensions holding them back. Reallocating their time, talent and treasure for multiplication is painful because the resources necessary for church planting compete with the resources needed to fuel the addition-growth activities they've become addicted to.

Often, Level 3 churches are strong at corporate evangelistic activities and programmatic growth but weak on biblical disciple making. They tend to add disciples primarily through corporate, programmatic means rather than through relational discipleship, with disciples making disciples.

As we discussed in chapter 3, these churches have a strong bias to building addition capacity vs. building multiplication capacity. Addition capacity becomes the primary means for adding disciples. Level 3 churches are strong at mobilizing volunteers for church service, but weaker on mobilizing disciples as 24/7 missionaries into every corner of society. For them, volunteer mobilization is vital to feeding the addition capacity-centered activities that fuel addition growth, with virtually no emphasis on mobilizing people in their uniqueness and calling for purposes outside the church.

Tensions: The tensions that hold these churches back from Level 4 are rooted in an operating system and DNA that optimizes addition activities to the exclusion of multiplication. Addition-focused operating systems are so deeply embedded in these churches that it would be difficult (if not impossible) to create the level of change necessary for Level 5 multiplication without overhauling the church. For this reason, a more reasonable first step for a Level 3 church is to aspire to and move to Level 4.

From 3 to 4: The move to Level 4 plays to the strength of a Level 3 church. This shift is programmatic and does not require deeply rooted change. Level 3 churches can actually program their way to Level 4. They simply need to embrace the journey to Level 4 with the same diligence and commitment as conquering the next growth hill. If your pathway is 3-4, you'll need to:

- Adjust your scorecard to include multiplication dimensions.
- Embrace multiplication beyond local multisite expressions.

- Treat church planting/multiplication with the same intensity as any other major new initiative or priority.
- Reallocate financial resources to multiplication.
- Set goals for church planting.
- Consider raising up and releasing leaders to plant churches, including encouraging staff to think about planting.
- Join a church-planting network, engage via your denomination, and/or affiliate with other churches that seek to plant churches.

The most direct path to Level 4 is churches themselves practicing the principle of first fruits, giving the first 10 percent of their income to church planting; encouraging their best staff and volunteers to leave and plant churches; and committing valuable time and leadership capacity to direct involvement in church planting.

To get to Level 4, Level 3 churches must shift and reallocate some of their programming resources to church planting and multiplication.

Level 4 to 4+

Level 4 characteristics: Level 4 churches make up approximately 4 percent of all U.S. churches. These churches have already made the programmatic shift to allocate their time, talent and treasure to church planting and multiplication. At a minimum they invest financially, often at least 10 percent of their tithes and offerings to church planting. These churches are committed to church planting and tend to press for increased involvement among the laity.

Tensions: Level 4 churches continually live in the tension of wanting to increase their church-planting activities but feeling the strain of resourcing their local church operations and growth. These churches recognize the importance of biblical disciple making and that the natural fruit of a strong disciple-making culture is a pool of leaders willing to go and be part of starting new churches. However, like Level 3 churches, they still struggle with weak disciple-making systems. The lack of strong biblical disciple making is a distinct tension holding back Level 4 churches from Level 5 multiplication.

From 4 to 4+: Although the shift from Level 4 to 4+ often happens naturally over time, Level 4 churches can expedite this shift by being strategic and intentional. Churches moving from 4 to 4+ always have a vision larger than growing their local church. They see their church through a Kingdom lens rather than seeing the Kingdom through the lens of their local church.

At the heart of transformation of Summit Church in Raleigh, North Carolina, from addition to multiplication is the idea of sending, says Planter/Pastor J.D. Greear:

"We've grown to be the sort of culture where sending is in the very air we breathe. Being a disciple means being sent; so sending should pervade *every* aspect of what a church does. First-time guests should know from the moment they set foot on our campuses that sending and Kingdom are in our blood."[4]

Churches moving from Level 4 to 4+ typically demonstrate an increasing number of the following types of behaviors:

- Reproduction happens through discipline, intentionality, and a multiplication strategy.
- Reproduction occurs at various levels, including multisite and church planting. However, these churches are more aggressive with their church-planting strategy than their multisite strategy.
- Their scorecard includes multiplication activities such as the number of churches planted; number of church planters trained; percentage of income allocated to church planting; and number of leaders deployed.

- They regularly celebrate multiplication wins, highlighting the impact of the churches they start and leveraging the opportunity to inspire others to be involved.
- They give sacrificially to multiplication, contributing their first fruits (both money and leadership)—typically at least 10 percent of their tithes and offerings.
- Decision-making and resource allocation are still strongly influenced by Level 3 demands. But these churches also have a demonstrated commitment to multiplication. They allocate resources to specific multiplication practices such as leadership internships/residencies; support services for church planters; participation in and affiliation with church-planting networks or associations; and direct funding of church planting.
- A healthy and active leadership development pipeline fuels the Level 3 activities of the church, as well as church multiplication.
- Releasing staff is more intentional compared with Level 3, where it is often reactive. In moving to 4+, releasing key staff becomes more intentional and frequent.
- Multiplication is typically more deliberate and planned than it is spontaneous, and often occurs with staff and interns. These churches are just starting to see lay people respond to God's call to "go" and be part of church planting.
- They are as passionate about releasing and sending as they are about accumulating and growing.
- The congregation sees church planting as a Kingdom-focused activity of the church that requires sacrifice.
- They have a bias to "go"—with a high value of mobilizing people in their area of giftedness and calling.
- Leaders regularly call church members to join and be part of church-planting teams, including the sacrifice to move to a new city or state.
- Senior leaders have a natural "holy discontent"—often resulting in a bias toward Level 5 behaviors.
- They've hired a full- or part-time staff person to oversee their church-planting activities.

- Their reputation for church planting is growing, attracting outside leaders who are interested in church planting.
- They tend to start local church-planting networks or affiliate with existing ones.
- Competition is no longer other churches, but instead the obstacles to increased multiplication.

New to 4

New church characteristics: Most new churches define their success using the prevailing Level 3 scorecard. They launch at Level 2 or 3 and spend several years struggling to become financially self-sufficient. Church planters tend to focus on the perceived stability of a Level 3 church, significantly influenced by the prevailing belief that at Level 3, a church is "successful." The various church lists (Fastest Growing, Largest, Most Innovative, etc.) are powerful shaping factors for new church planters. The average church plant does not have a vision for Level 4 or 5 multiplication. Instead, they embrace the "someday" philosophy: "Someday, when we can afford it, we will get involved in church planting." Unfortunately, for most churches that elusive day never comes.

During their first five years, most churches struggle financially, often bouncing between Level 1, 2 and 3, and always uncertain about their future. Most remain at Levels 1 or 2 (with many closing their doors) while some emerge at Level 3.

Tensions: For churches seeking to launch at Level 4, financial stresses are the top barrier. Their commitment to the principle of investing their first fruits in church planting uniquely distinguishes them from 99 percent of all church plants.

From New to 4: New church planters seeking to launch at Level 4 embrace that vision during their church's pre-launch. They commit to implementing as many Level 4 behaviors and values into their DNA as possible—making tough, risky decisions that buck prevailing wisdom. They know that the behaviors and decisions they make during the launch phase will ultimately shape and direct their future. They step out on faith to invest financially before it makes sense or before they can afford it. From the start, they commit the first fruits of their time, talent and treasure to church planting; get involved with a network/denomination to immediately help plant other churches; and they seek church-planting residents/interns who will go and plant churches within the first few years of their launch. Churches in this pathway plant pregnant. They commit to the following types of behaviors:

- Tithing to church planting.
- Launching pregnant with a church-planting intern or resident in place.
- Planting their first church before launching their first multisite.
- Planting their first church within the first three years after launch.
- Planting their first church before buying land or taking on mortgage debt.
- Setting goals for church planting during their first three, five and 10 years.
- Joining or affiliating with a church-planting network or denomination.
- Prioritizing church planting, building it into their bylaws and founding documents.
- Seeking to hire staff with the potential to plant churches.

The concept of "planting pregnant" became a reality for Revolution Annapolis planters Josh and Sarah Burnett. As they began to work on their staffing plan for the church they would plant, the only non-negotiable was a church planter in residence. Two years into launching Revolution, the church sent out their church planters in residence, Scott and Amber Ancarrow, to plant The Foundry in Baltimore, Maryland.

Burnett shares his story in the free eBook *Plant Pregnant: Leaving a Legacy of Disciples*. "If we're going to actually see a movement of church planting happen in America, then church plants will have to step up and plant pregnant. And the churches they plant will need to have the same DNA and conviction to plant pregnant.[5]

Like Level 3 churches that move to Level 4 or 4+, these new churches can move to Level 4 programmatically and without strong biblical disciple-making systems in place. However, unless they build into their DNA a balanced approach to the three dimensions of multiplication (disciple making, capacity building, and empowering mobilization), moving to Level 5 is an almost impossible feat.

New to 5

As I've said before, Level 5 multiplication requires a new operating system and wineskin. Because they don't have to overcome the resistance of changing existing DNA, new churches offer the greatest potential for creating new Level 5 expressions of the future. They have the freedom and flexibility to try new approaches.

Level 5 churches dream big and expect God-sized results.

Tensions: The greatest challenge here is the lack of models and examples in the U.S. church to learn from and emulate. That's why I turned to Ralph Moore, who leads one of the few Level 5 church movements (Hope Chapel) in the United States, to learn about the factors vital for launching at Level 5. Moore says new churches must:

- Build into their DNA simple, reproducible systems and processes that are accessible to the average Christian.
- Make disciple makers. More than 90 percent of Level 5 multiplication is solid, biblical disciple making, Moore

says, because the fruit of healthy disciple making is multiplication.

- Create a scorecard that values and celebrates multiplication.
- Focus on a leadership development pipeline that releases and sends out leaders, producing multiplication via new churches rather than simply fueling local growth.
- Instill a Kingdom perspective with big goals rather than local church perspective limited to local goals.
- Champion a strong bias to bi-vocational marketplace pastors.
- Start with and continue to raise up humble, yet tenacious, Level 5 leaders who can and will surrender their own egos.
- Live with an urgency and conviction that hell is real, and that those around us are dying spiritual deaths.

Additionally, below is a list of Level 5 characteristics Dave Ferguson and I presented in *Becoming a Level Five Multiplying Church*:

- Level 5 churches would have to *try* not to multiply. Multiplication is deeply embedded in their DNA.
- Multiplication seems to happen spontaneously and isn't limited to paid staff.
- Level 5 churches mobilize the priesthood of all believers to live deployed lives as 24/7 missionaries in their individual, unique corners of society.
- Biblical disciple making is strong, with much of the church's growth occurring as disciples making disciples who make disciples.
- Strategies are simple and reproducible.
- They have a different scorecard rooted in sending and releasing capacity vs. adding and accumulating.
- They have a solid balance of the fivefold gifting (Ephesians 4) with a strong apostolic impulse.
- They develop an aggressive intern and residency program (leadership development pipeline leading to church plants).

- They focus on pastoring and transforming a city/geographic area versus building and growing a church.
- They allocate significant financial resources to macro-multiplication (e.g., greater than 10 percent of their tithes and offerings).
- They routinely release staff and members to planting.
- Every disciple is a potential church planter/team member.
- Daughter church plants carry the multiplication DNA and are also active in church planting/sending.
- Decision-making and resource allocation always happen through the lens of church multiplication.
- Multiplication activities and commitment transcend the tenure of the senior pastor.
- They routinely release and send marketplace/lay leaders to plant churches.
- They regularly tell and celebrate stories of multiplication and impact.
- They regularly call members to sacrifice financially to church planting and are as inclined to run church-planting campaigns as they are church-building campaigns.
- They create and sustain systems to develop, deploy and support church-planting leaders and teams.
- They regularly coach and help leaders outside the church who are planting churches.
- Leaders are often founding members or part of a church-planting network or association.
- They develop best practices for others to follow.
- They strike a solid balance between addition-capacity building and multiplication-capacity building;
- They have an abundance mentality with a big vision for impact beyond the walls of the church.
- They are "spiritual fathers" to children, grandchildren, and great grandchild churches.
- They lead with a "movement" mentality.[6]

Additionally, Level 5 multiplication integrates the three dimensions of multiplication, the 10 characteristics of Level 5 churches, and the five shifts required for Level 5 multiplication. To see a Level 5 movement of multiplication like Moore's Hope Chapel, we must include all of these factors into our vision and plan. Ralph Moore is collaborating with SEND Network Vice President Jeff Christopherson (members of our Becoming Five team) on an eBook focusing on the "New to 5" pathway. Look for this new resource in early 2017.

Level 1 or 2 to 4

Level 1 and 2 churches live in a scarcity culture underneath continuous stress, causing them to focus on Level 3 as the solution. In some ways, the Level 1 or 2 church experiences many of the same dynamics as those in the "New to 4" pathway. However, the new church often has external funding for several years.

These churches have three pathways to Level 4:

1. First, like a new church, Level 1 or 2 churches can faithfully commit to investing the first fruits of their time, talent and treasure into church planting and multiplication. Just as we teach our members to tithe regardless of their financial situation, churches should do the same. However, their scarcity culture and financial reality make this commitment difficult. It is a very tough pathway, but the key question for Level 1 and 2 churches aspiring to Level 4 is, "Will you put Level 4 behaviors in place even when the financial and human resource balance sheets suggest it's impossible?" One prudent path is to take the list of Level 4 behaviors and simply "downsize" it to smaller steps and/or choose a few items to focus on and pursue.

2. Second, a church could follow conventional wisdom and wait until they can afford it. Of course, the biblical foundation for this path is weak, and the elusive day of investing in church planting rarely ever comes when taking this pathway.

3.   The third option is to focus on getting to Level 3 in a way that can springboard the church to Level 4 using the "3- 4" core pathway (described above). Churches that follow this path must understand and grasp the reality that many of the strategies for getting to Level 3 create roadblocks to moving on to Level 4. If you're serious about Level 4 and take this path through Level 3, be cautious in embracing Level 3 behaviors that actually hinder Level 4 progress.

Levels 1, 2, 3, or 4 to 5

For most churches, the new operating system that Level 5 requires will only be possible by shutting down for three to six months and relaunching, using the "New to 5" pathway. Practically, we know that this means most existing churches will focus on moving to Level 4 (or 4+) rather than Level 5.

However, Level 3 and 4 churches do have the resource base for experimenting and piloting new expressions that may help create new pathways for existing churches moving to Level 5. For now, we have yet to discover the pathway needed to move existing churches to Level 5.

Ready, Aim, Fire!

Hopefully, you're feeling equipped with the knowledge and insight needed to develop a plan for multiplication and to set out on your specific pathway toward multiplication—or to at least identify your pathway and what you'll need to do to prepare for the journey. However getting to where you want to go not only takes knowing your current location, your future destination and your pathway, it also requires you to get serious and make a plan. Without the non-negotiable step of planning, vision and pathways are nothing more than cool-sounding concepts that we dream and talk about, yet never put into action.

It's time to move!

Chapter 7
Planning
How Will We Get There?

*Good planning and hard work lead to prosperity, but hasty shortcuts
lead to poverty (Proverbs 21:5).*

Are you ready to move forward? Do you understand that your core
purpose and legacy is making biblical disciples? Do you get that a
vision for multiplication starts with discovering God's dream and
vision and then building your vision around His? Have you taken
the time to begin formulating your unique vision? Do you have
perspective on where you are today and how you got there? Have
you identified a key pathway for multiplication?

Are you ready to move toward Kingdom multiplication and the
dreams God has for you and your church?

Then this next part of the journey is key to awakening those
dreams and keeping them alive. To get where you want to go, you
must plan for the journey. As much as we love to hear about
overnight success stories, the truth is that planning and hard work
are the predecessors of fulfilled vision. When you declared your
college major, you planned what classes you'd need to graduate
with that degree. When you planted your church, you selected a
launch date and worked the details leading up to that first service.

The same is true as we move toward seeing the fruition of our
multiplication vision. We must plan to get there. The process of
planning and developing a strategy helps us begin to put this
futuristic abstract concept of vision into concrete action.

Why Should You Plan?

Knowing how to keep your God-given vision vivid and vital is one
of the most important yet neglected tasks in ministry. You may

know that planning is important, but the process of planning and developing a strategy to get where you aspire to be offers key benefits to everyone involved. With those benefits in mind, you can keep planning a front-burner priority, avoiding the rescheduled meetings and distractions that often throw us off course. Take a look at how planning really does bring you closer to the destination:

Planning nourishes your soul. Leaders who develop strategy for getting to their destination experience deeper personal meaning. As you reflect more on God's vision for your ministry and develop a strategy for moving in that direction, you'll start to see your vision as less of an insurmountable summit and more as a series of God-given checkpoints along the way.

Planning changes the scorecard. Because of the overwhelming strength of the "culture of addition" in the U.S. church, multiplication leaders get stuck and may not be giving themselves permission to more forward with a new perspective and definition of success. Planning invites everyone to the table to help change the scorecard.

Planning helps you focus your resources strategically. Two years ago, Will and his team at Auxano conducted research to find the greatest need for clear vision and strategy. He found that the No. 1 reason leaders want to remove the fog of the future is to know where and how to focus their resources. Your ministry time and ministry dollars are a precious, limited resource. Where will you direct the finite supply that God has given?

Planning aligns activity with priorities. Are the efforts and energy of your hardest-working people moving you toward your multiplication vision? Or does all of the activity and hard work seem more like running on a treadmill? They're sweating hard but actually going nowhere. Some companies call it the 80/20 Rule—80 percent of the efforts (unnecessary, unfocused and inefficient steps) yield less than 20 percent of the valuable outcome. Planning identifies the forward-moving priorities and the activity necessary to meet them.

Planning establishes direction and specific priorities. You and everyone on your team have a long list of responsibilities. The planning process helps each person know what he or she should be putting their energy toward—and what they should be working on first. The opposite is a group of talented individuals working on their own priorities that may or may not be actual work that moves you toward your specific multiplication dream.

Planning gets everyone on the same page. What would have happened if all 12 of the spies sent to check out Canaan would have embraced Joshua's and Caleb's perspective and realized that God had already given the Israelites the land? Having everyone on the same page is vital. Planning brings the team together as everyone works in unity toward the vision. At the same time, people begin to see how their individual role and daily work fit together to execute the vision.

Planning simplifies decision-making. My guess is that your church has a string of opportunities and new ideas consistently coming at you. Knowing what to say "yes" and "no" to can be difficult. When the vision and strategy are clear, those decisions become easier. Planning pinpoints the direction and activities necessary for success. When potential ideas and opportunities don't align with your multiplication vision and strategy, it's an easy "no." A specific strategy helps avoid distractions and gives you and the team the power to make decisions faster. I (Will) like to say, "The easiest measure of sustained clarity is the ability to say 'no' repeatedly, and to feel good about it."

Planning equips you to communicate the strategy and lessens frustrations. Have you ever worked with someone who keeps his strategy locked inside his head? He has communicated the vision, but no one except him knows the strategy for getting there. The planning process—actually talking about the strategy with your team and getting it out of your head onto paper—not only keeps *you* focused, it also gives everyone around you the necessary information and empowerment to carry out the strategy using their unique gifts and skill sets.

Planning helps you track progress. Without a strategy, you have no way of knowing if you're moving toward your vision. Key to any plan is the ability to create checkpoints and then gauge where you are. In fact, go back to our GPS analogy. A plan is like a map. You can always see how much you've progressed toward your goal and how far you are from your destination. Think back to our discussion on perspective in chapter 3. Planning gives you perspective. Knowing where you are on your pathway toward multiplication is essential for making good decisions on where to go or what to do next. At any time, you can refer to the plan and ask: What isn't on track? Why? What help or guidance can I give? What priorities do I need to reinforce? Planning answers the question, "Are we moving toward our vision?"

Planning uncovers potential problems. At each checkpoint, planning gives you discernment to identify not only the current problems but also potential problems in the future. Every road will have bumps along the way. When we identify and prepare for a potential problem, we give ourselves physical, emotional, and financial margin for responding to it versus reacting to undetected issues. The more prepared you are, the better you're able to handle problems as they surface. Or even prevent them by discovering solutions before they become a reality.

Planning extends flexibility. It may seem counter-intuitive, but having a strategy in place actually gives you the flexibility and margin to respond to inevitable changes. For example, if a team member leaves, you can review the plan and make the necessary adjustments. When everyone knows the guiding strategy, large shifts aren't as earth shattering as they might be without the planning process intact.

Planning tightens team execution, collaboratively. There are basically two kinds of church teams: those that get along and those that get things done. Rare is the ministry team that does both. In the process of building a plan together, many teams crack the code on positive accountability. You can get more done and have more fun at the same time.

By planning smart, we activate the vision. So the key question is not *should* you plan, but *how* then should you effectively plan to awaken the dream.

How Should You Plan?

As we talked about in chapter 5, the key question for developing our vision is, "Where does God want us to go and who does He want us to become?" So it makes sense that the planning process to carry out that vision would also start with God and prayer.

The Priority of Prayer

God alone wants to reveal His plan for your church. Not only that, His strategy is to be assembled in such a way that it can be clearly articulated to others.

From the outset in any major undertaking, there is to be no mistake about the origin of vision and the plan to get there. Almighty God who told the prophet Habakkuk, "Write My answer plainly on tablets, so that a runner can carry the correct message to others," is the author of our church, our vision and our strategy.

In his free eBook, *Collaboration for Multiplication*, Houston Church Planting Network Founder Bruce Wesley shares the story of HCPN, whose vision is to be a "network of networks that exists to strengthen church planters who multiply churches to reach every man, woman and child in the greater Houston area." In addition to supporting church planting through collaboration, the network has launched the HCPN Church Planting Residency to fund, train and support church planters who will hopefully become movement makers in Houston. All of it, Wesley says, started on a foundation of prayer, as pastors throughout the city began to learn about the common ingredients of spiritual revivals sweeping through some global cities.

"Unified prayer and multiplying church-planting movements were two key ingredients," Wesley writes. "In Houston, church leaders spearheaded prayer meetings and retreats to ask God to transform our city. God used these prayer gatherings to tear down racial and denomination divisions in the city."[1]

In downloadable resources referenced in their 2016 book, *God Dreams* (B&H Books), Mancini and Warren Bird offer specific prayer exercises for your vision team.[2]

When we let God carry His vision, His way, we will see the One who called us, the One who is faithful, and the One who will complete the vision. Only the Creator of the universe can give you a mental image followed by an understanding of the pathway toward the splendid future He has planned for you and your church.

Understanding the Role of Leadership

"Leadership is the capacity to translate vision into reality."

In his weighty quote, leadership scholar and author Warren G. Bennis summed up the leader's role in this planning process. Your role is catalyst—a person precipitating a change. Equipping yourself for this vital role you play is key to seeing you and your church's multiplication dreams realized.

One of the key things you can do as a leader is to make sure that *you* have a crystal clear picture of the multiplication vision. Have you come together as a team to really spell out your church's unique multiplication vision? Does the team share a powerful picture of the future? To get there, you must carve out some time. Where there is no margin, there is no imagination.

Realize that your vision has a cascading effect on everything else. Cloudy visions foster blurred and confusing priorities, frustrated employees, and disappointing results. Sharp visions foster clarity and powerful momentum. Think of the vision in five parts defined by five specific questions:

1. *What are we ultimately supposed to be doing?*
2. *Why do we do it?*
3. *How do we do it?*
4. *When are we successful?*
5. *Where is God taking us?*

If you haven't thought through all five aspects of your church's vision, your team won't be able to access it.

If you asked these five clarity questions to the top 40 leaders in your church, what would they say? If they don't have a clear, concise and compelling answer that's the *same answer*, then you know there's work to be done. In the course of planning, leaders are responsible for what I (Will) call "vision dripping." Throughout your daily leadership, you "drip" vision to the team. Over time, that vision begins to sink in and saturate others who also begin to drip the vision.

Vision ought to be a team sport and engage an army of everyday storytellers. It should never be relegated to a special gifting that only the point leader can share.

Six Reasons Why Plans Fail

With any dream we pursue, the journey will have inevitable roadblocks to navigate and pitfalls to avoid. Sometimes we can get a better picture of what to do when we look at the opposite scenario— what *not* to do. Have you ever been part of futile meetings or a strategic retreat that was all talk, no action? All of the plans just stayed on paper. No one wants to spend their energy and time leading or being part of something that never takes flight. Conversely, a well-designed vision process is one of the most exciting things to lead and experience. Consider some of the reasons the planning process fails.

The plan is filled with too much information. We've all seen those plans with five overarching objectives and 22 goals (if you haven't, be thankful). The problem with too much information is that the only person who benefits is the executive pastor type or board member with a high need for control. Having all of the objectives and goals listed in one place helps them feel good about the plan. The real problem is that no one else in the organization cares much about the goals. A plan buried in information misses the human element and doesn't connect on an emotional level. It doesn't help the average person know what to do and how their work fits into the plan.

At the summary level, a plan should have five things: mission, values, measures and "vision proper" (everyone knows the one, most important goal at any time).

The plan's mission and values statements are too generic. Remember that we talked about generic vision being one of the obstacles to a Kingdom-advancing multiplication vision. Here it is again. We have been so saturated with "generic" in church leadership that we don't even realize what it is anymore. Mission and values should be broad, meaning ample, vast, extensive and large, but not generic. They are broad because they require many types of activities to accomplish them and many different kinds of tasks can flow out of a deeply held value. Your mission and values should be broad yet specific.

The plan doesn't clarify how the mission is accomplished. This goes back to identifying vision-advancing initiatives and determining the priorities and then responsibilities to get there. Everyone must have a clear picture of the vision and how their role fits into it.

The plan doesn't clarify when the mission is accomplished. Working toward something with no way of knowing if you've actually accomplished it can be frustrating. Plus, it can stunt progress. With no clearly defined criteria in place, urgency falls to the wayside. We are wired to work toward a goal. When we don't define specific criteria to work toward, other immediate tasks, often unrelated to the vision, start to push out vision-related initiatives.

The planning process involves too many people. Decisions by committee are often cumbersome and time-consuming. I'm not saying don't involve your leadership team. People own what they help to create. However, I encourage leaders to narrow the number of leaders involved, especially in the beginning planning stages. Then present the plan to the team, encouraging open discussion.

The plan is too rigid. The temptation will be to cling to the plan with an iron grip and even fight to protect it. But things will change and not go as planned. True visionary leaders hold their plans with an open hand. During his presidential administration, Dwight D. Eisenhower said, "In preparing for battle, I have always found that plans are useless, but planning is indispensable." Fixating on the plan causes us to miss warning signs of potential landmines we're headed into.

Vision Planning Exercises

As you start to think through the multiplication pathway you identified in the last chapter and develop a specific plan for moving from one level to the next, I (Will) want to offer you some practical exercises that you can do both personally and with your team. The supplemental *Dream Big Workbook* includes a series of exercises on planning. These exercises will put you on the path to developing a plan and creating momentum toward your unique vision for multiplication.

Knowing why you're doing what you're doing (our core mission of disciple making), where you're trying to go (your unique multiplication vision) and how you're going to get there (your pathway and vision plan) are essential in your journey toward Kingdom-focused multiplication. But are you personally ready to begin this journey?

exponential.org

Chapter 8
Penitence
Are We Ready?

"Truly, truly, I say to you, unless a grain of wheat
falls into the earth and dies, it remains alone;
but if it dies, it bears much fruit." ~ Jesus

The word "penitent" means the resolve to change, or repent,
because of the sincere conviction of guilt for one's wrongs. When
considering whether or not we're personally ready for
multiplication, we must first ask ourselves some difficult
questions: Am I ready to change? Am I deeply convicted that our
addition-growth focus falls short of God's bigger dreams for me
and our church? Am I ready to repent and allow God to have
control of the future?

Exponential doesn't take the turn toward multiplication lightly. In
fact, nearly every pastor that has made the move from Level 3 to
Level 4 speaks of a "death" of some kind. Perhaps it was the death
of a personal scorecard. Or a death to the fear of what others might
say. Or the death of a paradigm of vocational ministry. In his free
eBook, *Flow*, pastor and author Larry Walkemeyer shares his
personal story of dying to his internal scoreboard.

"In my own journey, it has been a radical shift to transition my
internal scoreboard from 'size' to 'impact,'" he writes. "This shift
is ongoing because my ego has a tendency toward perpetual
resurrection. Every pastor has to die to the scoreboard. If we settle
for the 'good' of addition, we will miss the 'great' of
multiplication. We will prioritize our reputation, our new
buildings, our church's depth, our church savings account, our user
friendliness, our squeaky clean systems and our committed staff
over the harvest."[1]

Our lust for addition growth is deeply embedded in our sense of self worth and the value of our ministries. Consider how many pastors greet each other: The question, "How are you doing?" usually has little to do with real concern about that pastor's well being and is really more about, "How many are you running in weekend gatherings? Are the offerings up? Are you growing in numbers?"

Mac Lake, visionary architect for NAMB's Multiply network, calls it an "addiction to addition." This addiction, he says, can be one of the greatest factors limiting a church's expanding influence in their city and world. Lake identifies five signs that we've become addicted to addition:

1.   We're more concerned with expanding seating capacity rather than sending capacity.
2.   We're more concerned with how many people are in groups rather than how many people are leading and multiplying groups.
3.   We're more concerned about how many show up to serve together at one time rather than how many we can empower to serve 24/7.
4.   We're more concerned about how many people are "following me" rather than how many people are "leaving me" to go to lead a movement of their own.
5.   We're concerned only about our community or our sphere of influence rather than the world and the nations.[2]

Our practices are so wedded to our particular theological heritages that it can be painful to try to pull them apart. Overcoming this addiction requires us to repent to be released from the wrong scorecards, wrong strategies and wrong visions.

Perhaps as you've read through the first few chapters of this book, you're beginning to realize the magnitude of the shift from an addition to multiplication culture. The perspective you're gaining about where you currently are and where you want to be illuminates a gulf that may seem insurmountable. That perspective is also likely spotlighting the inadequacy—even the brokenness—of your current visions and strategies to get to multiplication.

But, while perspective produces understanding, understanding enables repentance.

True repentance is a deep, heartfelt conviction about turning from what we now know is wrong to what we understand to be right. Here are at least three types of repentance that could come into play independently or collectively:

1. **Repentance for ignorance:** *(Oh God, forgive me, I didn't know.)* As we grow in our faith, we learn more and more about God, realizing things we never knew before. Perhaps that's how you feel about gaining understanding on the difference between addition and multiplication.

2. **Repentance for unbelief:** *(Oh God, I knew that about You, but I chose not to believe.)* Sometimes we give mental assent to a principle such as, "God will take care of me," but in practice, we actually live in a way that suggests we don't believe God can take care of us. Think about the response of the distraught father as he begged Jesus to heal his demon-possessed son. When Jesus told him, "Everything is possible for one who believes," immediately the boy's father exclaimed, "I do believe; help me overcome my unbelief!" (Mark 9:24). In the same way, to see Jesus heal us (and our church), we need to confess and repent from our unbelief.

3. **Repentance for rebellion:** *(Oh God, forgive me, restore me, help me to obey.)* We recognize that while we knew and believed what God showed us, we still chose to rebel. Our repentance is no less passionate than David's plea for forgiveness in Psalm 51 as he cried out, "Have mercy on me, O God, according to your steadfast love; according to your abundant mercy, blot out my transgressions."

105

Below, we've prepared a short guide for confession and repentance, adapting the 12 steps from the national Christian ministry <u>Celebrate Recovery</u>[3] to help you apply these steps to you and your church. Take time to prayerfully own the repentance in each one.

12 Steps of Surrender and Recovery

1. I admit that I am powerless over an unbalanced approach to growth that is biased to addition vs. multiplication and that our church has been pursuing an incomplete scorecard. I know that I cannot make the change without God.

For I have the desire to do what is good, but I cannot carry it out (Rom. 7:18).

2. I have come to believe that God can restore us and will reveal to us right motives for (and approaches to) healthy multiplication.

For it is God who works in you to will and to act according to his good purpose (Phil. 2:1).

3. I make a decision to turn our fears, failures and incomplete scorecards over to the care of God.

Therefore, I urge you, brothers, in view of God's mercy, to offer your bodies as living sacrifices, holy and pleasing to God—this is your spiritual act of worship (Rom. 12:1).

4. I will do a searching and fearless moral inventory of myself.

Let us examine our ways and test them, and let us return to the Lord (Lam. 3:40).

5. I admit to God, my leadership team, and my congregation the exact nature of my wrongs.

Therefore confess your sins to each other and pray for each other so that you may be healed (James 5:16).

6. I am entirely ready to have God remove anything contrary to a healthy and balanced culture of biblical addition and multiplication.

Humble yourselves before the Lord, and he will lift you up (James 4:10).

7. I humbly ask Him to remove all of my shortcomings.

If we confess our sins, he is faithful and will forgive us our sins and purify us from all unrighteousness (1 John 1:9).

8. I ask for forgiveness from our congregation and from any past or present staff that we have selfishly held on to, and am willing to make the changes necessary to move toward multiplication.

Do to others as you would have them do to you (Luke 6:31).

9. I have made a firm commitment and am ready to take specific, intentional steps to give increased priority to multiplication.

Trust in the LORD with all your heart, and do not lean on your own understanding. In all your ways acknowledge him, and he will make straight your paths (Prov. 3:5-6).

10. I continue to take personal inventory and when I am wrong, will promptly admit it.

So, if you think you are standing firm, be careful that you don't fall! (1 Cor. 10:12).

11. Through prayer and meditation on the Word, I seek to improve my conscious contact with God, praying only for

knowledge of His will for our church and me, and the power to carry that out.

Let the word of Christ dwell in you richly (Col. 3:16).

12. Having had a spiritual experience as the result of these steps, I will commit to carrying this message to others and practice the principles of multiplication in every aspect of our church.

Therefore, having put away falsehood, let each one of you speak the truth with his neighbor, for we are members one of another (Eph. 4:25).

We began this chapter with Jesus' words from John 12:24. In verses 25 and 26, Jesus goes on to say:

"Whoever loves his life loses it, and whoever hates his life in this world will keep it for eternal life. If anyone serves me, he must follow me; and where I am, there will my servant be also. If anyone serves me, the Father will honor him."

The martyred German evangelist Dietrich Bonhoeffer made the sobering statement, "When Christ calls a man, He bids him come and die." Bonhoeffer's words set the stage for our crucifixion. Jesus bids us to come and die. In dying to self and our own desires, we are called to serve God. It is how we are faithful to Him and why He honors us. That is how Kingdom multiplication happens.

Now, just pause. Take time to sit back and reflect. Are you free from the shackles of your past? What baggage will continue to limit your effectiveness in moving forward? What unresolved issues do you have? I encourage you to go back through each of these steps and count the cost. Are you ready to make the necessary decisions and live sacrificially? Is it time to take action and move?

Chapter 9
Priorities
What's Important Now?

*"Plans are only good intentions unless they
immediately degenerate into hard work."*
~ Peter F. Drucker

If you're feeling overwhelmed, you're in good company. Two
thousand years ago, a team of learners felt the same way. They
were grieving the loss of their Founder and one of their 12 team
members. They felt uncertain of themselves and their future.
Clearly, they were squarely at Level 1 (subtraction culture), unable
to see any forthcoming movement.

While simply giving up would have been the easiest response, the
11 disciples pressed on in faith, taking one small, determined step
at a time. Then Jesus showed up in Jerusalem to give them their
mission—"Go!" And then, "Wait." Wait for what? They knew
their assignment. What did they need to wait for?

*"... wait for the gift my Father promised, which you have heard me
speak about. For John baptized with water, but in a few days you
will be baptized with the Holy Spirit ... you will receive power
when the Holy Spirit comes on you; and you will be my witnesses
in Jerusalem, and in all Judea and Samaria, and to the ends of the
earth"* (Acts 4:1-8).

In the first two chapters of Acts, we see how the disciples took
steps to carry out Jesus' Great Commission, both before and after
Pentecost. They waited for power, prayed, put the right leadership
in place (Mathias replaced Judas), held to the authority of
Scripture, shared the gospel, called people to action and lived in
common, modeling what they would ultimately multiply.

As leaders, we can learn from the disciples and create specific priorities with concrete short-term actions that move us toward multiplication. Like the disciples, we need to rely on God's power (not ours), pray diligently and proactively, hold fervently to Jesus' commands, put the right leaders in place, call people to a higher standard, and model what we seek to reproduce. These actions are vital and non-negotiable.

As you've learned by now, the pathways to Levels 4 and 5 require intentionality, courage and discipline. There's a reason why 96 percent to 99 percent of U.S. churches are currently at Levels 1-3. To become a multiplying church, we must redefine our success based on Levels 4 and 5, learning to shift our focus from attracting and accumulating to releasing and sending. We must acknowledge that the priorities and behaviors we're comfortable with also constrain us to Level 3 or keep us plateaued (Level 2) or in subtraction mode (Level 1). Bottom line, carrying out Jesus' multiplication dream requires action.

When I hear people talk about good intentions with no plan for executing them, I always think about this quote from Peter Drucker, the father of modern management: "Many brilliant people believe that ideas move mountains. But bulldozers move mountains; ideas show where the bulldozers should go to work."

If you're serious about moving to Level 4 or 5 multiplication, you must move beyond the inspiration of ideas or a vision. And that action needs to start right now. If you read this book and come away inspired or convicted, yet don't take specific, concrete steps to change, you won't see multiplication. It's as simple as that.

We must have a plan that moves us from good ideas to action.

As you finish this book and start to think through what it will take to turn your dreams into reality, here are a few suggested priorities:

Assess and gain perspective

1.   Take the Becoming Five free multiplication assessment (www.becomingfive.org) and then ask your team members to take it independently. Compare the results. Where are you like-minded? Where do you see things differently?

2.   Critically work through all of the exercises and tools in the *Dream Big Workbook* to assess how you're doing in specific areas of multiplication. What barriers do you need to overcome to get to a new level in each area?

   • disciple making (Honestly ask yourself, *Are we making biblical disciples that multiply or cultural Christians that consume?*)

   • capacity building (As your church grows, are you increasing Kingdom capacity for implementing new contexts for disciple making?)

   • empowering mobilization (Are you prioritizing releasing and sending? Are you equipping your church to discover and use their unique calling in ways that don't directly benefit your church?)

   • scorecard changing (Are you defining new measurements of success for you, your leadership and your church?)

Clarify and understand

3.   Seek to clearly understand the five levels of multiplication. The free eBook *Becoming a Level Five Multiplying Church* offers qualitative descriptions of each level.

4.   Reread chapter 6. Identify your church's primary pathway to Level 4 or 5. Make sure your team understands what this journey will require of them, both personally and in their respective ministry areas.

5.   Work with your team to develop a shared understanding of your starting point and where you'd like to be in three to five years. Seek agreement on the types of challenges and constraints you'll face as you move toward multiplication. Agree on at least three vitally important things that must happen for you to move forward.

Commit

6.   Decide if you're committed to the journey. Are you willing to make the personal sacrifice to move to Level 4 or 5? Ensure that your staff and leadership teams are fully onboard.

7.   Seek training/equipping for you and your team to help you move to Level 4 or 5. Exponential offers more than 20 free eBooks from leaders pursuing multiplication in their specific context (small church, networks, global outreach, etc.). Consider working through some of these books together.

8.   Attend an Exponential conference (choose from several live events throughout the year: Orlando, Los Angeles, Washington, D.C., Chicago, Houston) and/or work through the content in Exponential's Digital Access Pass, featuring the five main sessions from Exponential conferences plus additional live content.   Vist www.exponential.org/digital-access-pass.

Plan and implement

9.   Create a one- to two-page description of your 10-year vision for multiplication that brings the vision to life in full, living color. Include a list of specific, measurable characteristics, describing what multiplication will look like for your church in the future (e.g., tithing 10 percent of the

offering and any capital campaigns to church planting; planting at least three churches per year, establishing a church-planting residency, joining a church-planting network). Include in this description your new scorecard.

10. Create a "current perspectives," document identifying the characteristics of your current level of multiplication. Be specific and include the elements of your current scorecard. Note any specific factors from your past that have resulted in who you are today as a church. Finally, list any specific obstacles that currently hold you back and must be overcome.

11. Develop a plan, taking into consideration what you've identified about your current reality, your vision and your pathway.

Multiplication in and through your church *can* be a reality. Jesus doesn't ask us to do something for His purpose without empowering and equipping us with the vision and the plan for it. However, like anything in life, we can have everything we need but without action, good intentions are futile. Drucker offers another gem to remember:

"It is meaningless to speak of short-range and long-range plans," he said. "There are plans that lead to action today—and they are true plans, true strategic decisions. And there are plans that talk about action tomorrow—they are dreams, if not pretexts for non-thinking, non-planning, non-doing."

Jesus has called you to discern what's important and through His power create true, strategic plans now.

Endnotes

Chapter 2: Purpose

[1] Peter F. Drucker, Frances Hasselbein, *The Five Most Important Questions Self Assessment Tool: Participant Workshop* (Jossey-Bass, 2010), 7.

[2] Alan Hirsch, *Disciplism: Reimagining Evangelism Through the Lens of Discipleship* (Exponential Resources, 2014).

[3] Alan Hirsch, *The Forgotten Ways: Reactivating the Missional Church* (Brazos Press, 2009).

[4] Ibid

[5] Bob Roberts, Jr., *Real-Time Connections: Linking Your Job With God's Global Work* (Zondervan, 2010).

[6] Ibid.

Chapter 3: Perspective

[1] M. Scott Peck, *The Road Less Traveled: A New Psychology of Love, Traditional Values, and Spiritual Growth* (Touchstone, 2003).

[2] Reggie McNeal, *Missional Renaissance: Changing the Scoreboard for the Church* (Jossey-Bass, 2009).

[3] Jeff Vanderstelt, *Saturate: Being Disciples of Jesus in the Everyday Stuff of Life* (Crossway, 2015).

[4] Alan Hirsch, *The Forgotten Ways: Reactivating the Missional Church* (Brazos Press, 2009), 177.

[5] Ibid.,169.

[6] Jim Collins, *Good to Great: Why Some Companies Make the Leap...And Others Don't* (HarperBusiness, 2011).

[7] Jeff Christopherson, "The Kingdom-Centric Church Plant" namb.net/send-network-blog/the-kingdom-centric-church-plant

Chapter 5: Pursuit

[1] Henry Blackaby, Richard Blackaby, *Experiencing God* (B & H Publishing Group, 2014).

[2] Henry Blackaby, Richard Blackaby, *Spiritual Leadership: Moving People on to God's Agenda* (B & H Publishing Group, 2013).

[3] Jeff Sorvik, EFCA Church Multiplication Prayer Letter, November 2016.

[4] Matt Carter, video, 100peoplenetwork.org.

[5] Larry Walkemeyer, *Flow: Unleashing a River of Multiplication in Your Church, City and World* (Exponential Resources, 2014).

[55] Will Mancini, Warren Bird, *God Dreams: 12 Vision Templates for Finding and Focusing Your Church's Future* (B & H Publishing Group, 2016).

Chapter 6: Pathways

[1] Robert Frost, "The Road Not Taken."

[2] definition of pathway, thefreedictionary.com/pathway.

[3] Todd Wilson, Dave Ferguson, Alan Hirsch, *Becoming a Level Five Multiplying Church* (Exponential Resources, 2015).

[4] J.D. Greear, "Writing 'Sending' Into Your Church's DNA," jdgreear.com/my_weblog/2015/03/gospel-summit.html

[5] Josh Burnett, *Plant Pregnant: Leaving a Legacy of Disciples* (Exponential Resources, 2015).

[6] Todd Wilson, Dave Ferguson, Alan Hirsch, *Becoming a Level Five Multiplying Church* (Exponential Resources, 2015).

Chapter 7: Planning

[1] Bruce Wesley, *Collaboration for Multiplication* (Exponential Resources, 2014).

[2] Will Mancini, Warren Bird, *God Dreams* downloadable resources, goddrea.ms/resources.

Chapter 8: Penitence

[1] Larry Walkemeyer *Flow: Unleashing a River of Multiplication in Your Church, City and World* (Exponential Resources, 2014).

[2] Mac Lake, "Six Signs You're Addicted to Addition (And Why That's Not a Good Thing)," exponential.org/addicted-to-addition/.

[3] Celebrate Recovery, "Celebrate Recovery 12 Steps and Biblical Comparisons," celebraterecovery.com/index.php/about-us/twelve-steps.

Other FREE Exponential Resources on Multiplication

The following eBooks are available for free download via exponential.org/resource-ebooks/

Becoming a Level Five Multiplying Church by Todd Wilson and Dave Ferguson with Alan Hirsch

Spark: Igniting a Culture of Multiplication by Todd Wilson

Play Thuno: The World-Changing Multiplication Game by Larry Walkemeyer

Sending Capacity, Not Seating Capacity by J.D. Greear and Mike McDaniel

Launch Strong: A Planning Guide for Launching a Multiplying Church by Brett Andrews and Dale Spaulding

You Can Multiply Your Church: One Journey to Radical Multiplication by Ralph Moore

Flow: Unleashing a River of Multiplication in Your Church, City and Word by Larry Walkemeyer

The Journey: Toward a Healthy Multiplying Church by Darrin Patrick

Collaboration for Multiplication: The Story of the Houston Church Planting Network by Bruce Wesley

Sending Church: Stories of Momentum and Multiplication by Dan Smith

Together for the City: What Can Happen When the Mission is Bigger than 1 Congregation by Tom Hughes and Kevin Haah

Saturating Austin: A Strategy as Big as Your City by Tim Hawks and John Herrington

Igniting Movements: Multiplying Churches in Dark Places by Dr. Ajai Lall and Josh Howard

Reach: A Story of Multiplication in the City by Brian Bolt

More Than BBQ: How God is Creating a City-Wide Church Planting Movement in Kansas City by Dan Southerland and Troy McMahon

Give God Some Credit: Risk Taking for the Greater Impact by Brett Andrews

Start a Movement, Plant a Church by Josh Burnett

His Burden is Light: Experiencing Multiplication through Letting Go by K.P. Yohannan

Small Church, Big Impact: A Call for Small Churches to Multiply by Kevin Cox

The Question That Changed My Life: How Planting Life- Giving Churches Became Our Direction by Jeff Leake

Related Multiplication Resources

FREE eBooks

20+ new free eBooks are in our multiplication library. Authors include J.D. Greear, Ralph Moore, Larry Walkemeyer, Bruce Wesley, Tim Hawks, K.P. Yohannan, Ajai Lall, Brian Bolt, Jeff Leake, and many more. These leaders of multiplying churches share their journey of creating a sending culture of multiplication.

These eBooks are in addition to 60+ existing free eBooks in Exponential's resource library. Check out exponential.org/resource-ebooks to download these books.

Exponential Conferences

Don't miss the opportunity to gather with like-minded church multiplication leaders at Exponential's 2017 events:

Exponential East (April 24-27 | Orlando) and Exponential West (October 2-6 | Los Angeles) convene thousands of leaders and feature 100+ speakers, 100+ workshops, and nine focused workshop tracks.

Exponential Regionals bring the full punch of the national event theme in a more intimate gathering that helps leaders save travel expenses. 2017 Regionals will take place in Washington, D.C., Chicago and Houston, Texas.

Visit exponential.org/events to learn more.

FREE Online Multiplication Assessment

Discover your church's level and pattern of multiplication via our free online tool. It only takes 20 minutes to complete and is available at becomingfive.org

exponential.org

FREE Online Multiplication Course

The Becoming Five Course is designed to delve deeper into the practical elements of church multiplication. Leaders wanting to multiply their church will find valuable training in the form of audio, video, and written content supplied by dozens of multiplying practitioners, with the ability to work at their own pace. Visit exponential.org/register/b5-course/ to register.

Digital Access Passes (Training Videos)

Exponential offers downloadable content from all 10 main stage sessions via our Digital Access Pass (a separate pass for each conference theme) at exponential.org/digital-access-pass/:

2015: "SPARK: Igniting a Culture of Multiplication"

2016: "Becoming Five"

2017: "Dream Big: Discover Your Pathway to Level 5 Multiplication"

Connect with Exponential on:
Twitter - @churchplanting
Facebook - Facebook.com/churchplanting
RSS - http://feeds.feedburner.com/exponential

About Todd Wilson

Todd Wilson is co-founder and director of Exponential (exponential.org), a community of activists devoted to church multiplication. The international organization's core focus is distributing resources for church multiplication leaders.

Todd received his B.S. in nuclear engineering from North Carolina State University and a master's degree equivalent from the Bettis Atomic Power Laboratory. For 15 years, he served in the Division of Naval Reactors on nuclear submarine design, operation, maintenance, and overhaul.

After a two-year wrestling match with God, Todd entered full-time vocational ministry as the executive pastor at New Life Christian Church where he played a visionary and strategic role for several years as New Life grew and implemented key initiatives such as multisite, externally focused outreach, and church planting. His passion for starting healthy new churches continues to grow. Todd now spends most of his energy engaged in a wide range of leading-edge and pioneering initiatives aimed at helping catalyze movements of healthy, multiplying churches.

Todd has written/co-written multiple books, including *Stories of Sifted* (with Eric Reiss), *Spark: Igniting a Culture of Multiplication, Becoming a Level Five Multiplying Church* (with Dave Ferguson), and *More: Find Your Personal Calling and Live Life to the Fullest Measure* (Zondervan Publishing).

Todd is married to Anna, and they have two sons, Ben and Chris, and a beautiful daughter-in-law, Mariah (married to Chris).

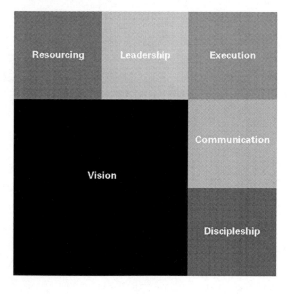

About Will Mancini

Will Mancini is the founder of Auxano, a growing, nationwide nonprofit church consulting group. As a recognized thought leader and clarity evangelist, he leads a team of "navigators" who help hundreds of churches each year to better realize their vision.

Will's previous work experience includes seven years as a chemical engineer and more than 20 years in ministry. A graduate of Dallas Theological Seminary, Will served as pastor of spiritual formation and leadership development at Clear Creek Community Church and FaithBridge, both in Houston.

In 2001, he jumped out of pastoring to start coaching and consulting full time after John Manlove Communications recruited him to build a vision clarity process for their church clients. After three years and incredible response to the visioning process, Will followed God's lead that would lead to the birth of Auxano in February 2004.

Will is also the creator of visionroom.com and the author/co-author of multiple books, including *God Dreams: 12 Vision Templates for Finding and Focusing Your Church's Future, Church Unique: How Missional Leaders Cast Vision, Capture Culture and Create Movement, Innovating Discipleship: Four Paths to Real Discipleship Results* and *Building Leaders: Blueprints for Developing Leadership at Every Level of Your Church,* among others.

Will lives in Houston with his wife, Romy, and his three children, Jacob, Joel and Abigail. Learn more about Will and his work at willmancini.com. Connect with him on Twitter at @willmancini.

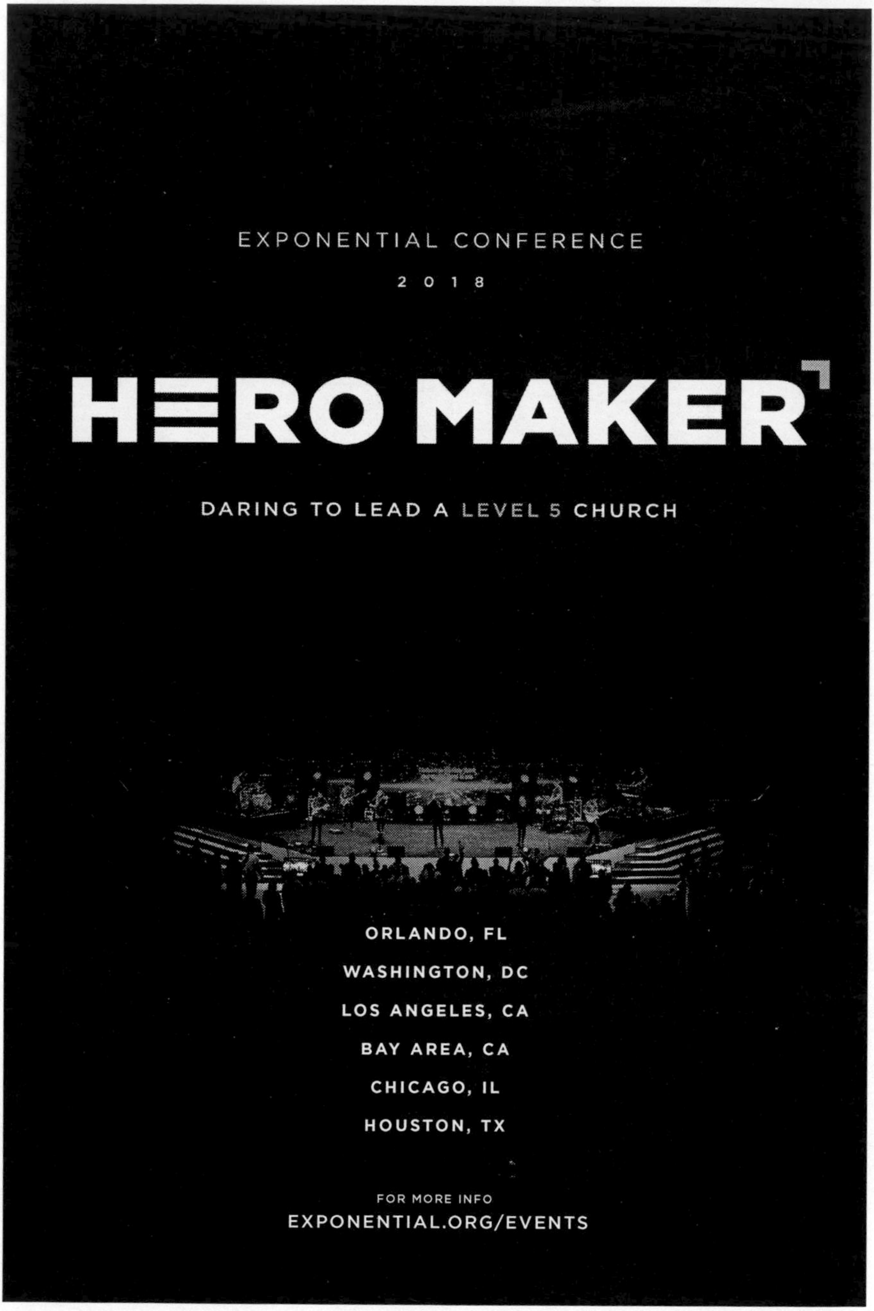
EXPONENTIAL CONFERENCE
2018
HERO MAKER
DARING TO LEAD A LEVEL 5 CHURCH
ORLANDO, FL
WASHINGTON, DC
LOS ANGELES, CA
BAY AREA, CA
CHICAGO, IL
HOUSTON, TX
FOR MORE INFO
EXPONENTIAL.ORG/EVENTS